v v v

Call My Name And
I'll Be There

v v v

Foreword

In a world that sometimes feels fractured and impersonal, poetry emerges as a testament to the enduring power of community. As we grapple with isolation or yearn for deeper belonging, our poems whisper a reminder - we are not alone. From the warmth of shared laughter to the hand extended in a time of need, our verses illuminate the many ways we find one another, sustain one another, and build something beautiful together.

Like a heart opening to new friendships across virtual thresholds, poetry reveals that we can share moments of laughter, insight, and vulnerability, even at a distance. These words become bridges, strengthening our connections both on and offline. In our poems we show the vulnerable truths, unexpected joys, and the deep well of emotions that makes us all human. We share pieces of ourselves and invite others to do the same.

This anthology invites you to explore the boundless landscape of community through the eyes of poets who understand its nuances, pains, and joys. Whether we gather around kitchen tables or in comment threads, in bustling city streets or quiet rural landscapes, this collection affirms that even the smallest gestures of connection can ripple outwards, touching lives and hearts in ways unseen.

Turn the page, and lose yourself in the world of connectedness that awaits.

Table of Contents

[Lliwen Jones]

Tea and a few musical notes

I sat there at the piano flicking dust,
while she made tea near a crowded sink
of dishes waiting for willing hands.

The boiling kettle was no distraction
for the fiddle and she held it
with precision, playing a Shetland air
that lit up her mind, leaving tea
far behind.

More tunes unplayed then
outside under a cold sun
her dog nestled warm against my leg

I stroked her slightly curly mane
sipping warm tea we spoke of melodies.

The sun still hovered
on the horizon as I drove
down the glorious lane
over the blue, blue lakes,
under telephone wires, past the flaming gorse,
a slate stepped path to nowhere
under that sinking sun
with a singing heart.

I'm a Welsh speaking Welsh woman from rural Wales with
nocturnal habits due to chronic pain. I'm often in a dream like
state at these times and the poems I write are often a surprise.
Allpoetry.com/Lliwen

[Michael Y.]

Crimson Leaf

Within the last chilly breath of autumn,
a single flaming crimson leaf
trembles for a final instant
before a savage icy wind arrives,
ripping it from its familiar branch,
tossing it randomly into swirling uncertainty

Wildly spinning in dancing circles,
the leaf tumbles downward
onto fiery wind-blown piles,
waiting in the still shadows of the forest
to be trampled into multi-colored powered dust,
where its nourishing rainbow atoms
flow with the first winter rains into the hungry earth,
replenishing the moist patient soil,
tingling the tips of wandering roots,
before rising upward
into the welcoming arms of towering oaks

Michael lives in Northern California with his Dearest Love and several pets. He has been writing for many years and hopes to continue writing and sharing his poems on All Poetry. Allpoetry.com/VanishingMike

[Marc Allen]

Have I told you how

it's 6 am and quiet,
nary the squeak of a hinge
in the house of doors.
Outside, all the bird-hearts
are perched on the top shelf
of sunrise
and the hiss and spit
of the coffee pot
sings a prophet song to sanity,
an homage to this other Eden
where a spell of good things
is a pearl buried deep
in the sting of yesterday,
an eastbound train
speeding in a western lane,
a book on how to build a boat
when the rain's already here.

Marc Allen resides in Lakeland, Fl. In addition to writing poetry, he always enjoys playing guitar, cooking and spending time with his family. He also raises chickens. Allpoetry.com/Marc_Allen

[Charles Carr]

Oh this old thing

It was the feeling of being exhaled,
rings of smoke giving up their shape, not as
a means to an end so much as bending
air back to breathe again; marriage became
a perceptible sense, an appendage—
the kickstand on a bicycle for two,
pieces of a puzzle—more form than fit,
the quiet work of light through cracks in less
than perfect lines: imagine horizons
anticipating sky, discovering
electricity in almost touching
skin; songs and dreams don't reach this far, it is
threading needles in the dark, a welder's
torch, the patient creation of a seam.

———————————

Charles is retired and lives with his wife of forty-four years and
counting in a house on a mountain by the river.
Allpoetry.com/selfrisinmojo

[Samantha Kriese]
Poetic Symphony

The violins strike a string
staccato.
A high note
keeps going.
The cello enters
vibrato.
Low note
continues.
Listen -
they confess a story.
The violins hold a long note
the cello chuckles two notes.
Silence.
The violins begin again
staccato.
Again the cello,
vibrato.
Listen!
Enchanting the listeners
with intoxicating sonority,
a poetic symphony.

––––––––––––––––––

S. A. Kriese resides in Chippewa Falls, Wisconsin. She is the author of 'One Who Plays with Paper and Pens' and 'In the Black Inkwell.' She has been featured in seven anthologies. 18 years of writing. Allpoetry.com/S.A.Kriese

[Ritwika Maity]

A poet isn't afraid of her voice

My dreams rise up, inky and wet,
blue, black and red - a testament
to all the bruises that birthed them.
They surround me, like smog at dusk,
and call me an imposter.
I tell them I'll write about it,
but the bile in my throat
chokes me.
Two decades of writing poetry,
from pencil tips to phone screens,
and now war has rendered me silent.

Concrete slabs weigh down on my chest
each breath is a countdown.
I'm afraid to hit zero.
Lives are grey dust, grey wind, grey skies
and whitewashed hope,
covered in scarlet déjà vu.
My birthday wish for world peace
would never come true
because peace costs a pretty penny
and poverty is free.
In my next life, then,
may I be born into another world,
more humane than my own,
more humane than my own.

Ritwika is from a crowded metropolitan city which offered her a diversity of stories and experiences she wishes to bring to life through her poetry. Allpoetry.com/Ajulea

[Subha Rajesh]

how war found him or he found war

dawn found them
yellow and orange
shining through the stained-glass panes
high roof a sturdy shelter
wife had risen with the ravens
aroma from the oven
testament to a breakfast sweet
some eggs too folded on plates
with love and sweat
he lived in field country
food and shelter done
had his warm clothes
for the winter coming
fortnights together
to turn the green white and grey

his hide, belly and head safe
wonders about his mates
future of his brood
how full is the treasure chest
what length the fields go
barrels loaded or not
now the enemy beyond lines
power and cash built they say

got worries now
keep him thinking
dreams of gathering his clan
find the guns and patriots
raid some neighbour
who might come spying
saw his neighbour's daring smirk
needs to talk to friends
ain't he the Senator
leader who snoops trouble
the one to gather soldiers
shoot the trouble's shoots young

the muzzle beads loaded now
will find the enemy's breast
some medals for his chest
then the peace that comes
with some coins and fuel cans
papers will be drawn
to put them in place
sighed as minutes now
remaining few grass on his scalp
turned grey in anticipation

will be losing young blood
and the children without a father
manifold will find foul ways
peace too his conscience whispered
yet what can I do
got food, shelter and clothes

now naught to do
but draw the imaginary trouble
poets found fantasy
he was no poet
a politician's brain
looks for fame and trouble
need the wars he said to himself
wars to keep safe
"can you cull me the chicken"
asked his wife
want them for the pie
just the line he needed
to convince his goodness away

blood on his hands
for his people's pies
all for the greater good
greater good, ha ha ha

———————————

This is Subha Rajesh from India.
Have always loved writing and poetry makes life meaningful.
Wars are as old as we humans and we still don't know when we
will evolve away this anomaly. Allpoetry.com/Bluewrite76

[Lonna Lewis Blodgett]

Rough Shod

A floor of dead rusty leaves rustle and crackle
Their crisp skins dancing under my feet
Shuffling with soggy soil thick with grit - I grapple
With sticky dew grass and spongy peat

Alligator-like tree bark grabs my hands then bites as I shamble
Holding on for balance on uneven chards of scalloped stone
Dazed by the cool dark mist in this early morning amble
I am rough shod but heart happy right down to my bones!

I am a lifelong poet, and live on the central coast of California. I
am a lover of nature and life, and a spiritual explorer. I write to
convey the quality of the human experience.
Allpoetry.com/Lonna_Lewis_Blodgett

[Walter Edvalson]

Written in Ink

Mary had straight hair pulled back and tied with lace.
She smelled of lemons in spring and snow in winter;
swore like a sailor when she was angry.
Two kids from a prior engagement
and a heart tattoo on her thigh;
the confidence of a hard life
written in ink.

I vowed I'd never leave, but trouble follows in the dark
like the click-clacking of a railroad track
or the barking of a dog.
There's a bus station in Denver
and a Trailways leaving at midnight.
Mary never even suspected;
it was written in ink.

Smoking two packs a day to whittle the hours away
in a jail cell in rural Mississippi
where even the moonlight offers no quarter.
Lying on a rotted cot
with a hole craved in my chest;
I'm dying to touch her tattoo again.
Mary was always written in my ink.

When I first started writing, a lot of what I wrote was in the form of lyrics, and to an extent, you can still see it in my style. For the most part AP Poetry has taught me a to be a better poet. Allpoetry.com/Thundrrd

[Gregory Espy]

Viet Nam A Love Song

Too far across the sea
in a place I'd rather not be,
on the winds of war ...
another day slips into forever.

I keep my head low,
pray Charlie doesn't know;
once again I'm running for cover.
The napalm flames get higher,
like an effigy on fire ...
burning down my high school memories.

I wonder if love still resides
in the places we used to hide,
or have they disappeared
into a jungle another world away.

The rapid beating of my heart
means another fire-fight is about to start;
the M16's fire through the dark
like a semi-automatic snare drum.

Another battle has begun
"Screw this hell hole" rolls of my tongue;
this is no way to treat any mother's son ...

Today have I learned what it means to die?
As mortar leaves the sky ...
the enemy have given their reply;
I listen to other men die
seems life all around me is failing.

If I ever make it home,
I plan never again to roam ...

get lost in her forever charms ...
and on the winds of love,
I promise we'll be sailing.

Hi, I am Greg from Memphis, Tn.
I was an English and Creative Writing Major in college.
My inspiration comes from the sights and sounds of my everyday
Allpoetry.com/GWE421

[Martin Rollins]

Miss Anne Thropes

Am I supposed to forget?
the world is burning
words are burning
pinions of flame like Phoenix
smite Drag story hours
and rise
that I might seem human.

Who am I?
A man in a sundress
getting railed by the train-
wreck of political discourse
while I glue my
ratty wig and curtsy
off the stage they built for
Miss Anne Thropes like me.

Am I supposed to forget?
schoolyard bullies whose words
like burning papers rip
off pages of my skin -
but I've got a story to tell
no less than the author who wrote
"It was a pleasure to burn."

Am I supposed to forget?
his hands no less than my hands
form fiery fists that beat my body but
I am more
than the pile of sticks he named me.

Martin Rollins is the openly gay Director of Sales for Real Estate Nexus, a New York poet, and community organizer. He is the founder and manager of Gayme Nite Rochester and Buffalo. Allpoetry.com/Martin_Rollins

[Scott E. England]

The Carriage Ride

On a countryside road I was traveling one day,
I espied an unusual sight by the way.

I might have passed by it, hidden there in the weed,
if not for the sense of my handsome young steed.

A quick jerk of the rein and I started to slow,
enough to make out what was there just below.

It seemed vaguely familiar, yet so out of place,
the sight of an arm and what looked like a face.

I felt sick to my stomach, and grew weak in the knees.
It was a body I'd found lying there by the trees.

From the bench of my coach, I couldn't be sure,
but the figure appeared to be that of a girl.

I pulled to the right and stepped down to the grass,
which had become the bed of this wayward young lass.

She was no more than a child, so innocent and pure?
I just couldn't imagine what she'd had to endure.

I reached out to see if she might've been dead.
I touched her sweet face from above her head.

She awoke with a start and she started to scream.
I saw fear in her eyes, which had long ceased to dream.

"I'm not going to hurt you," I said, trying to seem calm,
yet she cringed back away from the feel of my palm.

She shuttered and shivered and attempted to flee,
not knowing where she was, or who I might be.

Her panic was obvious, her confusion quite clear.
How did this child come to be lying here?

I searched for the words to reassure the poor waif,
but didn't know what to say that might make her feel safe.

Her long soiled hair lay loose on her face,
as if to defy what remained of her grace.

The rags that she wore hardly clothed her at all,
but told of the life that she led till her fall.

I returned to my coach to retrieve something warm
and attempted to place it around the girl's form.

She peered deep in my eyes in search of a sign
for some semblance of sanity that she'd hoped to find.

Fearful of me, she still had no trust,
her face now contorting in a look of disgust.

I could read in her eyes, she thought I was the one,
who did all the things someone else must have done.

I tried to relate how I'd found her this way.
That I wasn't the one who had led her astray.

She eventually listened and began to believe
that I might be her savior, her only reprieve.

I asked her name and she started to speak
in a voice that was shallow, raspy and weak.

I could barely make out the few words that she said.
"I think my name's Lisa", as she lowered her head.

"Well then, Miss Lisa, My friends call me Drew.
I live down the road just a mile or two.

If you think you're able I'll help you aboard.
That I came along you might thank the good Lord.

You may rest on my shoulder. We've not far to go.
What we do now from here my good Missus will know.

The size of her clothing should be just what you wear.
She'll tend to your wounds. You'll be quite cozy there".

She fell fast asleep no more time than it took
to drive down the lane through the gate, past the brook.

I gazed on in wonder at beauty replete,
collapsed there beside me in total defeat.

When the house just ahead gradually came into sight
I knew this young child was now safe from her plight.

She could rest easy in the care of my wife
and begin to move on with the rest of her life.

I reined in my rig and jumped down to the ground,
as I called to my wife to come see what I'd found.

She came in an instant, as I knew that she would,
and began to give Lisa the best care she could.

We helped her climb down and I carried her inside,
to whatever comfort that we could provide.

She had no recollection of how she'd come to be
on the side of the road to be rescued by me,

but she spoke of a baby that she'd left behind,
in the care of her mother, she needed to find.

She couldn't remember anything since that day,
beyond feeling helpless as she drifted away.

From that moment on everything was a blur,
until the moment she woke up to find me there with her.

We convinced her that right now she needed to rest,
and assured her tomorrow we'd all do our best.

We gave her clean clothes and made sure she was fed,
before my wife bathed her and helped her to bed.

Her family by now must be crippled with fear,
with no way to know that their child was safe here.

With our charge now asleep, we turned in for the night,
sure that we soon would set everything right,

but the thoughts in my head kept me tossing and turning,
in fear of the things that I might soon be learning,

about the young girl that almost lost her life,
and how she had lived through such horrible strife.

A long restless night offered me little sleep,
so I went to check in on the girl in our keep.

I opened her door by the dim light of dawn,
and peeked in to see that Miss Lisa was gone.

Thinking she might've stepped out for some air,
I checked the veranda but she wasn't there.

Her bed was unmade and the night clothes she wore
were lying in a pile in the middle of the floor.

I called to my wife to see if she'd know
what happened to Lisa or where she might go.

We searched the whole house and the entire estate,
from the woods and the meadow, out through the front gate.

We looked everywhere from the loft to the ground,
but the hapless young lass was nowhere to be found.

She must've been frightened and couldn't have known
she'd be as safe here with us as if she were our own.

I had no way to know where the girl might be,
but somehow I sensed she'd returned to the trees.

I hitched up the buggy and set off once more,
to the place down the road, where I'd found her before.

When I stepped to the ground on the grass where she'd laid,
there was something that suddenly made me feel afraid.

I couldn't explain it. Nobody was there.
It was just a cold feeling that hung in the air,

to fill up my nostrils as I inhaled each breath,
with the unmistakable stale smell of death.

Lisa had been there. Of this I was sure,
but as I looked around I saw no sign of her.

I stood there in silence, while scratching my head,
observing the ground that had been the girl's bed.

Kicking at the dirt, something odd caught my eye.
An out of place rock poking through toward the sky.

I found a sharp stick and I started to prod
at the stone I had found buried there in the sod.

It was almost a foot wide, about four inches thick.
It seemed to be some sort of very old brick.

The more I uncovered, the more I could see
what looked like some numbers and letters to me.

I could tell right away it was a stone from a grave,
that the soil having held it reluctantly forgave.

As I read the words that were etched on its face,
I became light headed, my pulse starting to race.

I sat on the ground and leaned back on a tree,
unable to grasp what was happening to me.

The stone told the story of a girl long ago,
who'd passed and was buried at the side of this road.

She'd been alive when our country was young,
but soon lost her life at age twenty and one.

The girl's name was Lisa. She had died giving birth,
and was returned to the Lord at this spot on this Earth.

The stone meant she'd come from a family of means,
accustomed to enjoying all of life's finer things,

but the one thing her money was unable to provide,
was for her soul to rest on the day that she died.

She was still searching for the child she had borne.
Never having held him before she was torn,

away from the baby she wouldn't get to love,
until they're reunited somewhere up above.

I tried to make sense of it. This just couldn't be.
She'd stayed at my house with both my wife and me.

I held her and carried her. She told me her name.
She talked with my wife. Am I going insane?

I prayed to my savior for some kind of sign,
to please let me know that I'd not lost my mind.

I couldn't explain it no matter how hard I tried,
so no more would I mention that strange Carriage ride.

I reset the marker and cleaned up her grave,
and looked after the girl I was too late to save.

Never again did I see our young guest,
but hope that I've somehow helped her spirit to rest,

and that someday, somewhere she might finally be free
to become the mother she never got to be.

I am a proud Hoosier and Army Veteran. Writing has always
been my escape and my go to method for dealing with the realities
of life, both good and bad. I love the rhyme.
Allpoetry.com/S.E.England

[Gary Rubin]

Red, White and Blue Summer Beach Vacations

It didn't take much to piss off my dad
behind the wheel of a humongous blue gas guzzler
our family car was a tightly packed sardine tin
two lane highways jammed with other tin canned sedans in our
way

Country Road faded in and out on the a.m. dial
agitation compounded by boyish giggles at the sight of
Coppertone billboards
dad drove with one hand, the other delivered a backseat back-of-
the-head haymaker attitude adjustment

Family road trips produced scrapbook photos
rail-skinny boys in clam digger shorts
women in one piece swimsuits, with oversized cat woman
sunglasses
men statuesque in plastic woven folding lawn chairs
rotund bellies sunburned bright red except for the white folds

Red, white and blue summer beach vacations

Gary is a married empty- nester, father of two adult daughters. He
is an outdoorsman and longtime resident of Wayland,
Massachusetts Allpoetry.com/GaryRubin

[Jessica C. Wheeler]

Revival

An old, forgotten piano
rests in stillness
anticipating
beneath a veil of dust

Glistening specks float
in beams of sunlight
dancing
to memories of melodies

Coated keys of black and white
preserved through fleeting years
waiting
for a renewal

She trails her finger through the dust
a clean black line follows
revealing
potential beneath neglect

The old stool creaks when she sits
a friendly sound
comforting
a prelude to a sleeping symphony

She hesitates, then touches a key
a note emerges
resonating
declaration of resilience

And with a sweep of her fingers
the settled dust stirs
rediscovering
her song

Jessica C. Wheeler is a writer from Branford, CT, where she resides with her husband and two young daughters. Allpoetry.com/Jessica_C._Wheeler

[Joe Brazeau]

Inside a Piano

the old upright player piano
tucked into a corner of the
den, books and magazines
stacked in sliding piles
across the top.

above the foot pedals
sliding doors opened
to reveal a space
for a 4 year old to fit
comfortably inside

crank the rollers to
start the music and quickly
slip inside, slide the doors
closed and lose myself
as the notes
flooded through my
vessels like a freight train
high on a rickety trestle
speeding into a dark
unknown tunnel but with solid feet
and firm grip as I run, the
piano pushing me on and
telling me it's the right way to go

fall, 1970 I found myself on a
bench next to my piano teacher
every saturday at noon for seven
years I hitch-hiked into town for
my piano lesson and then
thumbed a ride back home

brother Scott began
piano lessons within a year
he took a boogie woogie route
I was drawn to classical.

1974, Scott and I played a
duet of battle hymn of the
republic for the recital
our audience cheered

today I play the favorites
listened to
dozens of hours
remembering warmly
those days long passed
hiding inside the old
player piano in the den

Joe lives in Los Angeles Angeles. He has been a member of All
Poetry since 2008. He wants to expand his collection of poems to
publish in several books. Allpoetry.com/Joebraz

[Susan A Szoke]

caught in the open

rain trickles
down my body
cold...I'm so cold
droplets sit on my face, arms
coalescing in rivulets
streaming down
chilled skin
like hungry ants
scouting for food

dark green
in a face framed
with wet ringlets
I watch hope
slink away
without utterance
like an outcast mutt
I am isolated
wet
frozen
to the bone

a man shelters
some distance away
too close
for my taste

night air is rent
with the lonely outcry
of the midnight train
while the sleeping world
continues in silence

a stray flash of light
illuminates a wolf's outline
on the tracks
waiting...
for what
I wonder

as the storm intensifies
the man and I both dash
to the same place of safety
...that wolf doesn't move

in time we learned
of an abandoned truck
stalled
crossing the rails
...of a missing woman
police now searched for

the stranger said
that he like to think
that animal
was warning the train

for the truck's sake...
not likely, I thought

we left
before learning
its story
nor that
of the truck's
missing female

he headed
for his home

while I
slipped deeper
into hiding

———————————

GardenDelights is from Largo, Florida. She began writing poetry in late 2019, finds herself compelled to write almost daily, seeing it as having similarities with an addiction.
Allpoetry.com/GardenDelights

[Jacqueline Hird]

Icy fingers reach

Tips of icy fingers reach,
creeping to my folded skin.
It sits; forever pearly, til
spring bulbs bloom.

Yet every time, deposits build;
reminder of my own winter.
It eats away my clock,
turning spry blood blue.

I see, through frosted pain;
drifts of snow white hair,
with which children still play.
Tombed, body gives in;
shutting away, as wintery
snow.

Final flurries pass the stratosphere.

––––––––––––––––

My name is Jacqueline and I live in Perthshire in Scotland. I have
enjoyed writing poetry all my life. I have a particular love of
nature and try to spend as much time as I can in it for inspiration.
Allpoetry.com/Jacqueline_H

[Andrew Stull]

red cinnamon gum

I don't want to die
the way
my father's father
died.
he wasn't "grandpa"
he wasn't "pap"
he was just an old man
whose brain grew plaque
that murdered his memories
of cold bottles of beer
on hot summer days
and long nights
punching clocks
on the glass factory line.
he loved baseball
he loved his Pirates
he loved red cinnamon gum
maybe, he loved my father.
when his time came to die
he did so in a nursing home.
his tongue and lips
forgot how to speak
and his throat
became a lonely theatre
lined with rows of empty seats

made of splintered wood
that reeked of stagnant dishwater.
he died on a Tuesday
late at night.
he didn't remember my name
or the fact that he never loved me
and I never loved him.
when I die
I want my heart to give out
in my sleep
near some familiar sandcastles
while the ocean breeze
slips in through my bedroom window
as my sweet Lydia
battles me
for the last bits of blankets
covering our feet.

Andrew is an aspiring novelist and poet from Clarksburg, West
Virginia. He loves to travel and once drove six hours to Ocean
City, Maryland just to get donuts. Allpoetry.com/Andrew_Stull

[Bill La Civita]

Fireflies

cooking ribeye
smoke envelops this seaside cottage
with dark greasy bellows
the smoke detector's music
screams of our chthonic sacrifice
of fire and flesh to the god Poseidon

windows open
smoke wafts toward the stratosphere
we breathe out choking fumes over the cliff's edge
hypnotized by the surf's rhythm
and sparks of glitter floating
all around the cabin lot

We talked and watched
the diamond ring of streetlamps
and far-flung house lights
circling the far-away crescent shore
And we discovered fireflies'
radiant flashing signals

hovering lanterns
light August's teeming sky
waves scatter star power
onto seas lapping the foot of the bluff

where we sit towering together over
Truro's scrubby dune

A smile blazes across your face
and I marvel you are so enchanted
with these living beacons
and we almost fall back into each other's arms again

Firescapes of insects danced
through every twilight in distant childhood yards
I never focused on their magic
until those cool summer evenings
curled up on the heights with you
above Cape Cod Bay

_____

Poetry came back to me when I retired. I enjoy reading, history,
gardening and short get-aways with my husband Michael
Allpoetry.com/Blll

[Michael A. Mannen]

the solitary route

Life is a series of maze
sorrow hits everyone
the solitary route
value of granites, the stone
it's taking us back.
sparks of light are out
it is difficult to search,
the hidden exists.

Michael Mannen is a writer based in Kentucky and a graduate
from the Harvard School of Public Health.
Allpoetry.com/diamondsto01

[Jenni Taylor]

Puppy Seeks Pranks

He sits up,
the happy pup asks, "play a prank dad!"
Dad says,
"glad the funny lad wants a laugh!"

Due to a car accident in 2002, I am paralyzed from the neck down and vent dependent. Most of my poems are about me, my accident, hope, gratitude, for contests and life in general. Allpoetry.com/Jtay

[Stephen Harris]

Autumn is an old man

Autumn is an old man
who has sat for too long
in damp clothes
who's cologne is a wet open bark
foisty, woody
the breath of decaying leaves
he is the disturbed soil
sliced and squared
dug up peat
the wet wood burning
and the marshland muck
of mummified turning

––––––––––––––

I'm a train driver living in Wakefield, West Yorkshire where I can often be seen drinking coffee with pad and pen in hand. My poems tend to be autobiographical in nature. I hope you enjoy. Allpoetry.com/Atryst

[Jan Hayfield]

The box

The market is full of people
pushing themselves
past the stands.
I drift like a fatty
globule in vegetable broth.

Then I spot a blonde head,
over by the irises
strands fluttering in the wind.

I almost wave, my hand
already half raised
but then the figure turns.
I was so sure it was you!

And that's why I don't go anymore
to the park where we
read poems under the oak trees,
to the tavern
in which you held my hand
to the beach,
where the golden sunlight
wished us a good night.

'Cause you wait there
to give me another smile

nod to me;
once you winked
like to say:
"You're not alone."

It's starting to rain
and the market empties.
I'm still standing
at the potatoes
dripping wet and paralyzed.

From now on I'll stay home
until the fog has cleared.
Your things are all in one box.
The box, at the back of the closet.

Jan Hayfield is from Germany. He used to write short stories and
started to write poems in 2023. Poetry helps him to explore his
feelings, and to keep his mind off things.
Allpoetry.com/NovemberMan

[Andy Colin Clayton]

Travel

While I traveled along the way,
I saw a crooked man walk the crooked mile
and he said to me he was all alone
so I carried along on my way

―――――――――

We believe in one God, the Creator of all things. Heaven and earth shall pass away, but my words will stand forever. If we say we have no sin, we deceive ourselves and the truth is not in us. Allpoetry.com/Andyclayton728

[Alwyn Barddylbach]

Scarecrow on Brawny Down

Who vowed to nature's own in autumn crown?
A puff of woodland smoke the season vinified,
murder of mocking crows on brawny down.

Clogs of claggy fog soak a scrawny gown,
princely pauper's paunch of stolen rye,
poker face and beady eyed in autumn crown.

Hear the whimper ply with stubbly hat and frown,
stuffy head on rusty fork all mummified,
stoke and shock god's warbler on brawny down.

Goblin for a farmer's curse now tumbledown,
corn in gumboot onion parsley ossified,
needle teeth and bones of straw in autumn crown.

The poacher's game, the armoured night disowns
me, stalking skins and feathers mortified
while raptor, stake and pumpkin clones gawk on brawny down.

The ruddy meadow flourishes at sundown,
nursing ageing fruit and talk of damselfly.
Who vowed to nature's own in autumn crown,
to murder mocking crows on brawny down?

I bring you autumn's harvest, nature's own, my villanelle to scare
a lonely landscape, and a human or two - AB Blue Mountains
Allpoetry.com/Barddylbach

[Paul Goetzinger]

The Snow Moon and the Wolf

In February's twilight, Wolf howled
Moon listened
Above distant hills, he rose devouring the last rays of Sun
Wolf looked at Moon
His white complexion was a dull shade of red
Wolf asked if Moon was well
Moon told Wolf that he was chasing Sun through the sky
When he caught Sun, he was burnt all over his body by Sun's rays.
He was all red and in pain
Wolf said to Moon "This will not do, you must be white, so my
family can see to hunt tonight."
Wolf waved his arm, a chilling wind and a blanket of snow
approached from the north
Wolf gathered up the flurries and covered Moon all over his body
Moon felt relieved; the snow took away his pain and his white
complexion returned
He now lit the path for Wolf and his family to hunt
So, now when Moon gets too close to Sun, and turns red on the
eastern horizon, Wolf summons a storm and covers him with
snow to alleviate his pain and light the path

Paul Goetzinger is a freelance writer and educator from Des
Moines, Washington. He has written articles for magazines and
other publications for the past 20 years.
Allpoetry.com/Paul_Goetzinger

[Vanessa Ross]

When Breathing Is Easy

Lungs expand with oxygen like lavender
Black pants glisten with gold and brown fur
Cinnamon tea steams on the wooden table
A kitten purrs in my lap in sequence with each breath

A floor fan hums in July and provides a cool breeze
Olympic runners on TV remind me of my youth
Lined paper and a black pen speak through my steady hands
When breathing is easy...

_____

I feel things deeply, writing helps me express this. Animals have always been a source of comfort and inspiration. I live in Michigan surrounded by family and good friends.
Allpoetry.com/Vanessa_Kimberly

[Glenn Houston Folkes III]

Natural Scent

The flowers will bloom,
To be bright and beautiful,
They smell like perfume.

———————————

I love Dallas, TX! Cowboys fan for sure... I attend ACU for a
D.Ed. and want to be the best 21st-century beatnik. Big fan of the
Dead Poet's Society, also want to be a modern scop; Irish
heritage... Allpoetry.com/FylgjaofOdin5000

[Holly A. Heston]

Rock Star

You
are the wandering moon
while
I
am just one of
your many
lingering stars

———————

Holly started writing poetry at the age of 12 in a Creative Writing
Class and fell in love with putting beautiful words together to
compose a thought, expression or feeling.
Allpoetry.com/Holly_Heston

[Lonna Lewis Blodgett]

Guardian of the Heart

In the Spring
You are the untouched flowers
Booming within my youth
Providing colors and hues along
The pathway of promise

In the Summer
You are the sweltering heat
The fire of my desire and synergy
The sun at its crest of strength
The passion of my moment

In the Fall
You are the changing stillness
That softens the vigor of my declining intensity
Upon leaves in the wind soon fading from the trees
That stand rooted disrobing for the oncoming cold

In the Winter
You are the refuge for my emptiness
The harbor of my yearning that whispers
Hushed by the icy fingers of fate
marooned in isolating winds

You are the sweet pureness of friendship
Wherein the fates that I have suffered

You liberate my consequences with the truth
Of who I am to always be

By your side
I will never walk alone
You are affectionately a place for my heart
To find its home

———————————

I am a lifelong poet, and live on the central coast of California. I
am a lover of nature and life, and a spiritual explorer. I write to
convey the quality of the human experience.
Allpoetry.com/Lonna_Lewis_Blodgett

[Lisa Fiedor Raines]

God please take me now

Please take me home
To my lover, my love,
The other part of my heart

You took him too soon
A mortal wound to my soul
All I ask is to make me whole

———————————

AlisRamie is from North Carolina, USA.
Interests include: philosophy, history, international relations,
politics, poetry, art, design, jazz, funk, and some good old soul.
Allpoetry.com/AlisRamie

[Paul Crocker]

Connect With Me

My love, I wait patiently.
For you to come by and connect with me.
Autumnal leaves in the breeze.
But I know you'd never let me freeze.
With the connection that we share.
There is nothing we won't dare.

My heart, I feel you tenderly.
A warm pulsation that will connect with me.
The flowing of energy that never ends.
Beautiful moments that magically transcends.
With the connection that we create.
Our deserts are ready to saturate.

My one, I hear them clearly.
The words you speak that connect with me.
A dialogue sweeter than the angel's speech.
Sounding tones of which my heart cannot beseech.
With the connection that we tether.
We will always be together.

I am a poet from Bristol, UK. I started writing poems in 2001. I
enjoy both reading and writing poetry and everything connected
with it. Allpoetry.com/PoeticXscape

[Tina Thrower]

Longing for u

I sit here alone, .waiting for that moment for you to come back
home
The horror of complete loneliness
I feel rejected but know that not it at all
You are my sunshine
You make my days and nights
Waiting patiently just to feel your embrace and warm tender
kisses
Longing for you to hold me tightly and never say goodbye.

My world: I'm a mother and grandma, love the great outdoors,
bowling, watching movies and going on walks. I'm mainly just
trying to live one day at a time. Allpoetry.com/Icygreenleopard4

[D Grainger]
Crushing Footprint

A pinecone drops from the blue-green canopy that shields the
piercing rays of a golden sun.
It lay naked on the chocolate brown forest floor beside a baby
sapling.

The sapling's top is limp no longer stretches for the warmth of the
sun.
Its succulent needles rest in the crevices of a footprint.

Weeping echoes, unlike the gentle wind that whistles through the
limbs, it's a crackling and trampling.
It is not a rotting limb, pruned, falling to the forest floor, it's a
ripping and peeling.

Steps. Steps, like that of a thundering moose, etching footprints.
Snapping and crushing.

Forest shade and a canopy crumbles.

———————————

From Hawaii and now Washington. Write when the mind must
spill its spirits on paper. Yes paper! I am refreshed for days after
birthing a poem. Allpoetry.com/Darken_light

[Victor Étienne Windermere]

Sanctimonious Sandstorms

(Transformations of) Both Age [and Time]

"Time itself is not an illusion, but merely a construct of the mind that will bend, twist and stretch all according to our very own experiences and desires.

It is an ever-shifting non-Euclidean metaphor, where seconds feel like eternities, and years slip through our fingers like sand." — Victor É. W. | 2023

In this exploration, we delve into the intricate ways in which age shapes our perception of time, unraveling the threads that weave together our understanding of this intangible force. From the moment each of us enter the world, our relationship with time itself begins to evolve. The newborn, purely instinctual, perceives time as a sequence of immediate needs and responses, a cycle of hunger and satisfaction, sleep and wakefulness. There is no concept of 'tomorrow' or 'yesterday,' only the pressing urgency of the 'now.'

One

As that newborn matures into childhood, their perception of time begins to broaden. The introduction of structured activities like school and extracurricular pursuits impose the first tangible understanding of time. For a child, a week until a birthday party feels like an eternity. Each day seemingly is filled with a multitude of experiences and emotions, making time seem to stretch. The concept of an integer related to 'two weeks' (or more) now becomes a vast expanse to navigate, filled with more anticipation and impatience than a positive response.

Moving into adolescence however, the perception of time continues to shift in a different direction. The aforementioned adolescent, now slightly more aware of the wider world around them, begins to realize that time is but a finite resource. Days are filled with school, friends, hobbies, and perhaps a first job. Suddenly, time itself seems to speed up, moving faster than one seemingly would care to admit. However, our precious 'two-week' wait until the next holiday no longer feels like an eternity but a rapidly approaching deadline.

This acceleration only continues into adulthood. As responsibilities pile up—career, family, bills—the days blend into weeks, the weeks into months. An adult might feel that two weeks is hardly enough time to fulfill their obligations. They're constantly racing against the clock, trying to squeeze more productivity out of each fleeting moment. Time, once a vast expanse, now feels like a scarce commodity.

As we continue to age even further, transitioning into our later phases of development, our perception of time undergoes yet another glorious transformation.

This time; The days might seem long, but the years short.

The elderly often speak of time flying by, as they look back on their lives. Remember our 'two weeks' that once felt like an eternity? They are now, but a frantic race in adulthood and pass with a gentle, almost unnoticed rhythm.

Our perception of time, thus, is not constant—but indeed changes more and more as we age.

It is shaped by our experiences, our responsibilities, and our mental and physical states. Despite its unchanging methodologies, our relationship with time becomes fluid, ever-evolving, and mirroring each reflection we share with it as we continue our sojourn through the stars.

Two

Thus, as each chapter of one's life unfolds, so does the perception of time.

As it, too, becomes a never ending fractal, infinitely looping and repeating in unto itself with intricate purpose. With years beyond what we can perceive, the balance between ambition and reflection now comes into play. Reality itself dawns again, and again, as time is both a precious and infinitely non-renewable resource, and one hell of an elusive companion.

'Two weeks', a measure that once felt insufficient, now carries not only the weight of unfulfilled aspirations, but prompts a sense of urgency to make the most of every single passing moment.

Simultaneously, our understanding must deepen to see that time, while challenging, is not merely as simple as linear progression — But an effervescent, multidimensional idealism.
Memories, like delicate tendrils, intertwine with the present, blurring one's boundaries between past and present. That passage of time becomes less about measuring minutes, and more about savoring the richness of each human experience, relationship, and

core moment that has individually played a part in shaping their final journey.

Yet, even now as our knowledge allows time itself to seemingly slow in its passing, the awareness of its finite nature becomes more pronounced to each of us.

The knowledge itself that every moment is a fleeting gift, not only imbues a sense of bittersweet beauty—But our constant 'two week' metaphor, which once held both an infinite set possibilities for a child, and felt like a race against mortality for an average adult, becomes a reminder to savor each day, no matter what may come of it—To embrace the present, and the legacy we leave behind with gratitude.

As we continue to learn and grow as a species, we must come to ask ourselves; "What exactly does it mean to understand true essence? Does it lie not in measurement, or in the way that it molds us, challenges us, and ultimately defines us?"

———————————

Victor É. W. comes from a quaintly petite, yet humble township from Indiana, U.S.A.

Victor states; "Writing helps me to not only embrace my emotions, but to understand myself and others.'
Allpoetry.com/Victor_É._Windermere

[Lisa Fiedor Raines]

I remember your song

I had my white
Sunglasses on

Waiting for you
To see me smile
In the hot sun

My hair pulled back
Trying to look
So cool for you

We went driving
With the top down

My hair blew loose
In the wind

I miss those days
Of summer with our
Music playing loud

We were so hot
Senior summer

We were on top
Of our whole world

_____

AlisRamie is from North Carolina, USA.

Interests include: philosophy, history, international relations, politics, poetry, art, design, jazz, funk, and some good old soul.

Allpoetry.com/AlisRamie

[Courtney Weaver Jr]

Children

In our own world, we reside
A place where grown-ups can't abide
Too small for them to understand
Their minds unable to expand

They try to peek and poke around
With their eyes fixed to the ground
But they can't find the heart of it all
Where we laugh, and dance, and stand tall

Our lives are hidden from their sight
Underneath the cover of the night
In the closed flower, our dreams reside
And the eggs in the nest, where love abides

They may eavesdrop on our conversation
But they'll never grasp the fascination
Of our world, so pure and bright
Far from their reach, out of their sight

So let them wander in their own domain
While we revel in our world, free from disdain
For in the end, they'll never understand
Our small world, so unique and grand.

I'm a 66 year old male living in New Orleans. I started writing poetry again about a year ago and I find that it helps me process the everyday happenings in life. Allpoetry.com/Gray0328

[Georgios Kiminos]

The String Theory Of My Guitar

In the tapestry of my good guitar,
Strings, existence's wisps,
Weave the very fabric of a reality.
My fingers stretch unseen dimensions
No longer bound by the confines of mere particles.

For these minuscule strands vibrate,
A cosmic symphony in the unseen,
Each quiver, a verse in this celestial song,
Births a new refrain, a particle with its own tale.

Mass, charge, and spin dance in harmonious union,
Painted by the strokes of these ephemeral strings.
Solitary forces now waltzes with their counterparts,
Embracing the electromagnetism, weak but strong.

Hidden realms unfurl, tenfold or more,
These strings sway and intertwine,
Traverse, compact and veiled,
Beyond the reach of mortal gaze,
Shaping the invisible carpets of the multiverse.

In the realm of my super-strings,
Symmetry reigns supreme.
Supersymmetry, the elusive partner,

Dances with grace, a spinning tango in perfect accord,
Unveiling the deep profound Order.

In the crucible of thought, string theory births marvel untold.
The black guitar's hole tells its forgotten secrets,
Quantum gravity beckons and math and physics entwine,
dancing to the rhythm of these cosmic strings.

The unity among the diverse forms
Is now in front of us like a miracle explained,
And a La, an A, a holly sound, becomes the needle,
And the fabric knit by the fundament note is:
My membrane emerging cosmic symphony.

Oh, strings of my guitar,
Play the music of existence,
Harmonize the Theory of Love and Everything.
Reveal via your ethereal dance, from now on,
The universe's deepest truth,
Spoken in the language of vibrating strings.

———————————

I was born in Greece, and in my teens I started writing poems in
English, motivated by my English teacher. I earn a living as an ML
engineer but live my life with poems, lyrics, and music
composing. Allpoetry.com/Yiorg

[Martin Pool]

Bitter

A chocolate from the box smothers all other poor tastes looking
to soothe me
Tripping memories of the innocent child's mouth stuffed with
bon bons and of the less innocent
Tongue circling the nipple iced with melted Sees chocolate
cherries.

It is of course those trenchant and stirring memories of you that
linger.
Where are you now who are so distinct among the rings of my
life?
When they carve me up will they say there she is circa 1972?
Quite a year for him.! See his growth and then such
Withering and even nearly unto death.

The blessed silhouette hides my scar.
I cannot fully face those upon whom I let fall your shadow.
They cast about blindly, as waving beneath the bed for the other
shoe
Seeking my warmth and are cut.
Lingering at the threshold they slip notes rusty with old traps
beneath the door

I live inside a palisade, my face washed by the narrow wind
between the slats
Alert to smells entwined with our time.

A chocolate from the box, one dark and bitter, takes me on
another tumble.
I am small. At the mark. Smacking my lips.

Retired and reminiscing. Find I have a backlog of phrases looking
for an outlet and writing poetry has helped. I have read poetry for
most of my life and love the rhythm of poets like Dylan Thomas.
Allpoetry.com/Wantwallace

[Andrew Hatfield]

Invincible Young Man, Vulnerable Father

In youth's embrace, I stand so bold,
A young man's tale, forever told.
Nothing can halt, nothing can sway,
I'm invincible in the light of day.

No shadows linger, no wounds to bear,
In this moment, I'm free from despair.
I am a young man, nothing can harm,
A symphony of life, a carefree charm.

Yet, fate unfolds, and roles transform,
As fatherhood whispers, a quiet storm.
A child is born, a heartbeat new,
An echo that alters what I once knew.

Invincibility crumbles, vulnerability starts,
Through my children's eyes, life imparts.
No shield, no armor, love breaks the mold,
In their journey, my heart is enrolled.

I am no longer the invincible one,
Through each step they take, my journey's begun.
A father's strength lies not in the skies,
But in the reflections of his children's eyes.

Andrew Hatfield, a father, husband, and Soldier, was born and
raised in Vincennes, Indiana. He channels his expression through
poetry. Allpoetry.com/Andyhatfield20

[Maxwell Sebastian Burchett]

Betrayal

Only those completely trusted,
Can completely betray.
Trust gained at great cost,
The one treasure once lost
That can never be recovered.

Betrayal leaves a stain,
A shadow on the heart.
Trust once lost, rarely regained.
Never to return, faith and trust depart.

———————————

Max Burchett: a writer, singer and songwriter,
A crooner, a teller of tales,
A dream maker, soul shaker and captivator,
Hoping that in verse and prose he prevails.
Allpoetry.com/MaxBurchett

[Brian Sparks]

no oblivion

the sky wasn't scheduled
for a phlebotomy; out of blue,
out of the blue, the weathermen
read the forecast like prose-
lytes praying the rosary.

wine tasters judged the rain
and immediately forgot
how to dance, burned the roof
of their mouths on all the wishes
that welled up in the clouds.

likewise, you say, "all hugs
return to sender, someday";
our sensory output arriving home
from a kind of famine where
we become its last byte to eat.

out of space, we defragment
on some hard drive; the traffic
inside us having made inroads
until the streets had names;

names that scatter us
like light through blinds; tomorrow

morning, a shine of jail bars
giving the dark its own medicine.

———————————

Brian Sparks is from Philadelphia, PA and has been writing
poetry for twenty years, since his freshman year of high school.
Allpoetry.com/JackVanMeter

A new day

See the dawn,
Morning light,
Run away,
Feeling fright.

See the day,
Feel the sun,
Sleep it through,
Have no fun.

These are things that I do,
Can you see it from different view?

Taste the air,
Feel the wind,
Flying free,
You'll never bend.

See the stars,
See the night,
Take you over,
See no light.

These are things that I do,
Can you see it from a different view?

[John Campbell]

Hawaii Vacation

As we walk along the beach in Honolulu the sand welcomes our
feet
The warm sun and the gentle trade winds , are a combo not to be
beat
The waves brush up against the shore than offer a hasty retreat
A kite surfer floats across the water , looking so very elite
Surfboards with those tanned riders come rushing in
In an effort to impress those bikini-clad ladies , their hand they're
trying to win
Tonight a feast for the ages a luau , awaits
A romantic evening under the stars ours to create
Hula dancers swaying to the music under the moonlight
Drinks flowing like the ocean to liven up our night
Our evening of fun has come to an end
We leave in high spirits as tomorrow we will do it all again

———————————

John Campbell is from Victoria British Columbia. I have 11 songs
recorded in the U.S.A as the lyric writer. I use my poems as the
building blocks for the music . Allpoetry.com/John_Campbell

[Jim Beitman]

never to be found

never to be found
buried deep in the rubble
lives not forgotten

———————

I am an artist living in Noblesville Indiana. Writing is a great
media that helps distill my feelings, thoughts, and experiences. It
is always a great thrill to be included in an Allpoetry anthology!
Allpoetry.com/Beitmanjim

[David I Mayerhoff]

And Then They All Fell

The worker bees
buzzed and swarmed
while the Queen bee
hissed and barked

In each hive
the talk of the town
was how uninvolved
Queenie was
and even worse,
when she takes command
it is smooth
but passive and incoherent

The net result
was the workers
all snapping and hissing
at each other

More than one human
has been stung needlessly
over being in the
wrong place
at the wrong time

As more drones
were recruited into
this madness
the dysfunction
spiraled exponentially
out of all control

Everything in the nest
was bitter
even the honey

All of nature was effected
in a vicious cycle-
the flowers
were not pollinated

Gardens did not
sprout forth
the air was stale
from poor oxygenation

One big mess
all traced
to one single bee

Sadly the nature of the living
is to focus all the rage
on the immediate obstacle
and not on the ultimate cause

Easier to sting
the worker drone
next to you
who is building on your cone
due to poor hive policy
then to confront
the Queen Bee
in all her regal awe
and tell it like it is

Perfidy followed dysfunction
leading to all manner
of corruption and chaos
with all forms of violence
wreaked on the most vulnerable
who were least able to affect change

Like a contagion
other Queen Bees
saw how easy it was
to be lazy and disengaged
and this type
of dictatorial uninformed fiddling
while hives were burning
became the leadership style of the day
and spread anywhere where hive
civilization had reached

The few remaining hives
ruled by good governance

just leaders
and a sense of the common good
were the object of everyone else's
hatred, jealousy
and even violence

But then again
we are only
talking about bees
so why worry?!

———————————

David I Mayerhoff is a literary writer and poet, an established
scientific author and academic psychiatrist. He grew up on Long
Island and now resides in New Jersey.
Allpoetry.com/David_Mayerhoff

[Maxwell Sebastian Burchett]
Triad of Troubles

Some say, and believe, bad luck lurks in threes.
That a triplet of troubles and woes, even doom,
Can be expected to appear, joined in a trio for despair.

Bad luck, they say, unfolds in a three-act play,
With prologue, conflict, and ending, a trinity of troubles predict,
A superstitious claim and firm belief, that fate is to blame.

Three and three, fates agree,
Bad fortune looms, dooms in trinity.
Triple, triple superstition whispers, simple destiny.

———————————

Max Burchett: a writer, singer and songwriter,
A crooner, a teller of tales,
A dream maker, soul shaker and captivator,
Hoping that in verse and prose he prevails.
Allpoetry.com/MaxBurchett

[Lisa Fiedor Raines]

I'm sorry, Mommy

Maybe I just
didn't get the
lesson you were
trying to teach me

I may have said
something rude to
demean or correct you

Maybe I deserved
the backhand against
the mouth

But, now that you've died
I will never have
the chance to say

I'm sorry I hurt you
enough to strike me

I'm sure it was
all my fault

———————————

AlisRamie is from North Carolina, USA.
Interests include: philosophy, history, international relations,
politics, poetry, art, design, jazz, funk, and some good old soul.
Allpoetry.com/AlisRamie

[April Hamlin-Sache]

Tell It Like It Is

It was a Saturday afternoon when I broke up with you
I know it was too soon since I'm feeling all the pain
you put me through

Constantly reminiscing about us
me not being your first choice

I really loved you
you were all I could see
you were my everything

I remember when I called you to ask you to commit to me
that was the last time I heard your voice
now I only have a memory of
what it used to be between us

I wanted all of you
yet you denied me of your love from your heart

If only I had waited instead of jumping right in
we could have been friends with no end

I really messed up my life
you're the only one who could make it right

I miss you like you would not believe
I wish I would have conceived
carrying your sons inside of me

Although our relationship was short
you were mine
my longest genuine love

my reality
You are more than a dream
more than a fantasy

I was voluntarily your girl
in fact I approached you
without changing my mind

I genuinely wanted you without force or pressure
you were becoming my treasure

I will never forget about you
I am going to tell it like it is
you are real and true
not a fantasy
you are my reality

No fantasy or wanna be
you were truly with me
I was truly with you

This one is for you and me
a part of our reality

I am originally from Indiana. I have 5 poetry books, 2 books of short stories and 7 series on amazon.com. I am an Author and Admin Support worker who wants to Act/Write in the Entertainment Industry! Allpoetry.com/April_Sache

[Madelyn Paine]

Window Seat

I stare out the window
everything blurring out

My music is blasting,
can't hear a soul
only the internal screaming.

My mind wanders to the dark corners
I allow the loud thoughts to become louder,
too loud.

tap. tap.
"Can I sit here?"

His hair is curly and brown,
eyes a dull grey,
coat a bright red that's being soaked throughout,
boots with clumps of snow attached,
A fuzzy red hood,
covering his skin.

Thinking, unsure of my choices:
Should this boy sit next to me?
I want to have friends,
I want to have a life.

"no sorry, I'm waiting for a friend"

I go back to my music,
trying to ignore the screaming voices
questioning why I do the things
that I do.

Making up these silly scenes in my brain,
with the music.
it's tiring but rewarding,
letting them take over slowly
Drifting off to my happy place

This is my happy place:

flowers,
woodworking,
lemonade in the sun
on a hot, hot beach

I love my happy place

Faster than expected It's my stop,
I get off into the rain and snow
trudging home through the sludge

Staring at the house
a nice big roof,
slanted and black,
covered with glistening snow.

brown painted over beautiful wood walls,
brick at the bottom,

beautiful bushes and trees,
also covered with clumpy but bright snow.

This is my home.
stepping in,
I let the water and sludge drip off of me

Swinging off my bag,
take off my wet coat
kick off my snow-clumped shoes

I sit,
open up youtube
the screen is nearly as bright as the snow

I like the window seat
and all the comfort that comes with it

It's one of the only things that gives it

———————————

I'm a high school student in Canton, Michigan. I find great
happiness in poetry. I love expressing my interests and feelings
through my poems to share with others. Allpoetry.com/Poet369

[Gary Adcock]

a rockstar says goodbye

thirty years had passed since he had been back to his hometown
tonight to be his final farewell to a crowd that never let him down
the stadium, a sale-out, fans young and old there to hear him play
three decades his music capturing a world in an unforgettable way

bright lights and fast lanes found him when he was a young man
tour bus became his home on wheels, said goodbye to his old van
etchings in his face showed a life most would never get to know
if only people knew the many sacrifices in the making of a show

never made it home for services when his folks were laid to rest
called the funeral home each time to ensure nothing but the best
years of drugs and alcohol, it seems, took care of most his pain
memories fade in time if you don't let your heart drive you insane

as he pulls the mic up to his mouth a crowd erupts with every
word
chanting his name in unison, not noticing his speech slightly
slurred
a rockstar says goodbye that night, tears gently slide down his face
now begins a new life of solitude, hoping it's one he can embrace

the sound of tires bouncing off asphalt slowly putting him to
sleep
his destination this time final as his driver slows down to a creep
pulls up to an old familiar place, an empty house now rundown
thirty years had passed since he had been back to his hometown....

Growing up in the up in the Flint hills of Kansas I have always
been a dreamer. I love the outdoor and good music. When you
combine the two you have the makings of a great day!
Allpoetry.com/Gary_Adcock

[Tyler Atchison]

Under the Sycamore

In his disillusionment he decamps reality
To a place where his vexations turn to vacations
Where he may lie by the beauty of the sycamore
Full of twists, nature's masterpiece
As he lay debating on every notched branch,
He worries no more about his illness

The silky warmness
Which once filled his starry eyes
Returns, momentarily
All internal restlessness fades away
But, as he understands
His final breath is approaching

Mournfully,
The man longs to stay
For just one breath longer
Under the sycamore
Still the man pays his toll, and passes the Acheron
The river of those who were
In this moment of weariness
He slowly rests his heavy eyes
As he is now unbound to the beauty of this Earth

A young poet at only 23, and an Air Force Veteran. Poetry brings comfort to me, as I have been diagnosed with Bipolar Type 1. My only wish is my words touch just one soul.
Allpoetry.com/Atchison

[Catherine Mitchell]

Whispers of Faith

In life's tempest, where shadows loom, I've felt the weight of burdens, the impending doom. Yet within the depths of my soul's unrest, I find solace—a whisper of faith, a gentle quest.

Overwhelmed, I tread the waters deep, Anxious waves threatening to engulf my keep. But there, amidst the darkness, a glimmer appears, A beacon of hope, dispelling my fears.

Whispers of wind, soft and serene, carry me toward peace, where blessings convene. The path unfolds, a sacred thread, guiding my steps, where doubts are shed.

Spirituality weaves through every thought, A tapestry of grace, battles bravely fought. In this realm of unknowns, I navigate, through prayers and devotion, I resonate.

Faith, an anchor, steadfast and true, lifts my spirits, paints the sky anew. With unwavering trust, I release control, Surrendering to grace, my wounded soul.

Imperfect, yet held by love's embrace, my heart cleansed from worldly trace. In faith's sacred art, I find healing's start, A canvas of hope, a brand-new heart.

Let life's waves crash, relentless and wild, I stand firm, anchored by belief, reconciled. Beneath it all, a truth beyond grief, God whispers, "You're held I am your relief."

———————————

Catherine is from a small town called Ironton, Missouri. When she is not able to express her thoughts and emotions verbally. She writes them into poems hoping that it will help others.
Allpoetry.com/Catherine136

[Rebecca Baglio]

A little love

A little love,
From up above,
Clock ticking to win this race,
We are winning this race with love,
Hugs and kisses from thereof.

———————————

I write poetry and micro fiction on my micro fiction blog. I try to keep my micro fiction stories to a minimum of fifty words. I'm in a few anthology books for my poetry all ready. my name is Becka. Allpoetry.com/Beckey_Baglio

[Alexander Shaumyan]

In Our Great Republic

"The worst illiterate is the political illiterate."
--Bertolt Brecht (1898-1956)

In our great republic purporting to be free,
We have a choice of candidates: A, B, and sometimes C,
While both major parties are owned and corrupt,
We choose some lesser evil and boast we did our part,
Our part in rubber-stamping the tyranny of elites,
Who claim to represent us until their rule's complete.

Sometimes another candidate comes forth to rock the boat,
To actually take actions for which the people vote,
To end the wars and lawlessness of the entrenched deep state--
Such candidate inspires both loyalty and hate--
But that's the price of freedom, sometimes you have to fight
The oligarchs and the media for working people's rights.

They'll smear such a candidate with endless stream of lies
Of racism, homophobia, transphobia, as they try
To charge him with the crimes that they commit each day--
Those wealthy lying hypocrites fight to the death to stay
On top of wealth and power, where laws do not apply,
While people earn slave wages until the day they die.

I am a Russian-American poet born in Moscow, Russia, in 1962.
I've been living in the US since 1975. I enjoy poetry, foreign
languages, art, mathematics, chess, and drinking bourbon.
Allpoetry.com/Alexander_Shaumyan

[Samuel Miller]

My Fingers Drifting

A haunting mist
Lies o'er the keys;
Like satin sheets of creamy white.
I know not what to play.
In dusty, moldy corner sits
The object of my reverie:
My old piano, breathing still,
Heart beating almost silently.
I have not touched the keys in years,
Yet still they echo in my mind -
My fingers drifting through my dreams
In time with yesterday.

S. L. Miller is an aspiring poet from the Piedmont region of North Carolina. He spends his time reading, writing, and generally mucking about. Allpoetry.com/Cecil_Miller

[Scott Thrower]
Memphis, August 1988

Dank earthy August
lies hot upon the town

'round street lamps
the skeeters zizz

Dawn, iron and morose,
with rawboned, clammy fingers,
grips the dank city as
spider talons encircling
a dying fly

the great unwashed
the red of neck
white of trash
blue of collar

lurch forward on coffee and redbull
and contort angrily through another
Marlboro day.

—————————————

Voiceover artist and Registered Nurse, alive and medium-well in
Texas, USA, grandfather to Sunny, hiker, landscape
photographer, former resident of Los Angeles, Philadelphia,
Memphis, Portland OR etc. Allpoetry.com/Vox_Dude

[Kenneth Muldrow]

Dungeons & Dragons

Like the game, there are levels to this
Who are the dragons
The neighborhood predators
That torch you with illegal firearms
From the crown of your head
To the soles of your feet
Breaking up bricks
Like the Mario brothers
Flooding the block
With products and pills

These dragons are like their father
The Devil their tails are in front of them It's their lying tongue
taking out a third Of the community like the Devil took Out a
third of Heaven now
The hood is full of rogues and Demons

What's the dungeon the prison where The dragons and rogues go
And the warden and co.'s are the Warlocks they lock Away the
warring Barbarians labeled By society as Savages some Warlocks
use their Magic to oppress
And violate and some are consumed By their own magic imagine
a dragon Being trapped in the belly of The beast

Artificers bringing out capabilities in Objects like shanks and
anything That They can use to stab and bludgeon and Prison

tattoos made From melting Styrofoam or plastic And even
utilizing Ink from pens While they do time in the Pen some Go
into monk mode or seek religion
As well as the aid of the cleric going Through a crisis like sickle cell
while
Being sick of being in a cell

_____

My name is Kenneth Muldrow and poetry is my biggest hobby. I
have others like cooking, reading, anime, and hitting the gym, but
poetry is my favorite. Allpoetry.com/Zenith_Intellect

[Samantha Marie South]

Line Dance

Peg to line, the holder of clothes
Wind through cotton, the shirt tail blows
A dance ensues when breeze passes through
A sway of sorts, gentle and true

The waft of air through the textile
I sit, observe, and quietly smile
Beautiful nature and all its offerings
A wondrous thing

––––––––––––

Samantha Marie South lives in London. I have always had a
fondness for the written word which was rekindled during
lockdown.

Poetry provides a wonderful platform for expression of our
feelings. Allpoetry.com/Samantha_Marie_South

[Auto Fuentes]
A Fiddle's Grievance

You've played me like a fiddle,
Tuning me to be your very own.
You push and pull on my fragile strings,
forcing me to squeak out the elaborate melodies you've carved
into my soft flesh.

Oh, sweet player of mine.
Won't you leave me to dust in the dark and gloomy corner,
like all your other decrepit failures?
I see them covered in misty cobwebs,
swimming in the misery of your abandon.

I pray for the day you tire of my endless pitchiness,
The day you grip me by my neck,
Smashing my mahogany wood into your floors,
Camouflaging my remains with your matching wood panels,
So that when the rest of my rocky notes bleed out on the ground,
Nobody notices the missing mahogany fiddle from your endless
(and ultimately useless) collection.

Auto Fuentes is a teenage poet from Oak Forest, IL. Their works
are called 'bittersweet' by friends, and their writing is referred to as
'Lonely, even in the presence of the one [they] love (-S.I.D)'.
Allpoetry.com/Auto_Fuentes

[Courtney Weaver Jr.]

The Reality of Work

In the office lunchroom, sipping on my tea,
Chatting with a colleague, about what I see,
A reality TV show, with a plot so intense,
A reflection of our work, a perfect pretense.

There's a big house, filled with people in our minds,
Some are traitors, some loyal, in various kinds,
They don't know who to trust, who's playing a game,
Just like in our office, it's almost all the same.

The backstabbing, the deceit, the hidden agendas,
It's like a reality show, with no happy agendas,
We try to navigate, the treacherous waters,
But sometimes it feels, like we're lambs to the slaughters.

In the game of work, we're all players in a way,
Trying to survive, each and every day,
Some are traitors, some are loyal and true,
And we never really know, who is who.

So as I sit in the lunchroom, with my colleague by my side,
I can't help but see, the show and work coincide,
It's a reality TV show, playing out in real life,
And we're all just trying, to survive the strife.

I am 66-year-old male born and raised in New Orleans. Writing poetry helps me make sense of the things that happen in everyday life. Allpoetry.com/Gray0328

[Royce Earnest Rasmussen]

Survivor

In the caverns of my soul, echoes linger,
Whispers of survival etched in the silent spaces,
A tapestry woven with threads of resilience.

I am a wanderer of shadows, a survivor
Not born of battles visible to naked eyes,
But of wars fought in the recesses of a wounded spirit.

Each scar, a testament to the endurance of a flame,
Kindled in the crucible of adversity,
Burning through the darkest nights.

The echoes tell tales of storms weathered,
Of tempests raging within, unseen by the casual observer,
Yet the survivor wears no armor of victimhood.

In the labyrinth of memory, there are corners
Shrouded in the mist of ambiguity,
Where the echoes of abuse and illness intertwine.

I navigate the maze, tracing the contours
Of a narrative etched in enigmatic lines,
An autobiography penned with invisible ink.

The wounds, both seen and concealed,
Merge into a landscape of strength,
A survivor's silhouette against the canvas of existence.

I am the alchemist turning pain into power,
For survival is not a mere act of endurance,
But a testament to the aliveness that persists.

In the dance between shadows and light,
I emerge, not unscathed, but victorious.

Royce Earnest Rasmussen, a painter and poet from Rockford,
Illinois, USA, finds inspiration in the intertwining beauty of art
and verse. This marks his debut in the world of published poetry.
Allpoetry.com/Royce_Rasmussen

[Corey Parks]

Creation

What happens when "love" meets "pain" is the same thing that happens when an "unstoppable" force meets an "immovable" object.

A plausible course "outsourced " as a consolation, time stamped cancellation.

A "supernova" dedicated to a Galaxy freshly created, for life to begin, where atoms are separated in a "void" dark and spacious, where organic matter forms, ostentatious.in a sea of stars, where planets are weightless.

For life to begin, we must be patient. 75 words, to explain creation.

_____

I am a poet who loves writing about the things you want to say, but can't I want to leave a foot note in history for all to remember me. Allpoetry.com/Emerald_Titan

[Eyitayo Akintayo]

Nightmare

As I cupped my hand round
my Grandma's flowery tea mug
sipping hot Jamaican green
she made slowly, slowly, slowly
as the long day drawn into
darker night, laid myself to
sleep on the old worn-out couch
near the fireplace, soon began the
forty winks stuff.
Never in my entirety swam and not
willing to swim across the English
Channel to look for a true kiss so I
always say.

I had this dream or I should call it
a nightmare. What else!
My neighbourhood was churned into a
rage streets after streets flooded.
Found myself on a very big white van
to know you have to swim for it with a
strong current.
As I deep into the raging water I tripped
on something, knocking off my feet just
as the water going overhead.
I woke up not yet morning to start another
day chores and that was a dream on a good night.

A keen interest in traditional and folklore stories, at age 9 I scribbled on a brown paper a poem to my mother for the Mother's Day. Allpoetry.com/Davidponle

[Lisa Fiedor Raines]

A little time helps to lengthen the

perspective

It's been seven months now
November will be our eleventh anniversary

I remember the promises we made
We were to head to the Blue Ridge mountains

I'll sprinkle your ashes in the little pond
Out by the gazebo nearest the Blowing Rock

I'll stay at the lovely winery in Banner Elk
Where we got married and spent our honeymoon

I'll have brunch at the Village Cafe, and
Drive along the Blue Ridge Parkway

I may not able to walk much now, but
I must try to make it there for us

You keep me strong, my love, so
I won't be going alone

––––––––––––––––

AlisRamie is from North Carolina, USA.
Interests include: philosophy, history, international relations,
politics, poetry, art, design, jazz, funk, and some good old soul.
Allpoetry.com/AlisRamie

[Sean Cooke]

[The Real World.]

My eyes tell a story of a different world to yours.
My hands hurt from all the digging in the dirt.
You are consumed by social media.

I am a slave to fear.
You check to see how many likes you get.
I check to see if I can keep up with life,

The rain doesn't wash away my pain.
The wrinkles on my face, the calluses on my hand's, show how
I've wept and crawled across these unforgiven lands.

Your perfect photo has no wrinkles or eyes glaring with pain,
technology will take care of this so you will wait.

Your camera finally notices me but it's too late.

———————————

I am a 33 year old man from northern England, reading and
writing poetry is now a satisfying and productive part of my life. I
thank my mother and father deeply and all those who read my
poetry. Allpoetry.com/Arsenalfan30

[Sean E. Mallon]

The Moon's Path

The moon ushers in a translucent path

As I float across a sleeping ocean in a makeshift raft
Sharks encircle me with an evil-keel temperament
Whales bellow in sonorous tones

The air is frighteningly frigid
My teeth chatter sounds of fatigue
Water from the bottle is nearly drained
Crumbs are sparse

Stranded for nearly a decade on a desolate island,
I escaped a voiceless and empty life
Took by sea to reacquaint with the human race
May my friends remember me, and family embrace me

A dire death may arise by morning
But still, I drift towards the moon
On a path of sheer and relentless hope

Hailing from Saint Augustine, Florida, Sean is a family man, sport enthusiast, and avid reader. Like other writers, he wishes to communicate through the most delicate of art forms.
Allpoetry.com/Shamus_E._Malone

[David I Mayerhoff]

Split In The Moment

Mirth of daydreams
weepings of yesterday
moving ahead while pulling back
into the detritus of past spurned relationships
tepid investments and job loss

wail of the injured
the broken parts of us
step on the eggshells
of the damaged
while checking the rear view mirror
for oncoming traffic

A red light ahead
walkers crossing the walkway
as the engines of life
are afraid to stop
but pained to go on

If we just
roll down the window
we'll be given cups of water
to cheer us on
as joggers are gifted in marathons

Like the only guy living on an island
the solitary man driving within the car
passing so many autos on the road
with their windows rolled high shut

_____

David I Mayerhoff is a literary writer and poet, established
scientific author, and academic psychiatrist. He grew up on Long
Island and now resides in New Jersey.
Allpoetry.com/David_Mayerhoff

[Marcus Taylor]

I could be..

I could be lightning
I could be a star
I could be a black hole
way out there somewhere,
I could be your lover
I could be your sin
I could be the ending
Or where it all began,
I could be the ocean
Pulling at the moon
I could be the unborn
Swimming in your womb,
I could be lightning
Thunder in your ears
I could be the rain
Disguising brutal tears,
I could be a heartbeat
Singing out today or
I could be the silence
With nothing more to say...

———————————————

My name is Marcus Taylor born on the Isle of Sheppey
South East Kent, England. My passion is listening and collecting
progressive music of the 60s/70s but I enjoy writing poetry in all
its forms.
Allpoetry.com/Marcus_taylor

[Yu He]

Plum-blossom in Three Movements

Drifting beads of frost of the air.
Cantus slowing down the cold mountains near.
A ribbon of sound reverberates,
Mottled brights intercepting and crossing,
Giving multiple shade and change to the river well.
Tunes paint a fragile picture of the dusk.
As the world is clad.
The colours come tumbling down.
Playing with the lyre,
Blossoms taking flight from strings,
They are fluttering unknown visions on their wings.

Fluting on the drum-tight shell of topped snow.
How to compose for the balm in the cool wind.
Fresh snow scattering unequally on old ice.
Filled with heart-stirring highs and euphonious lows.
Enmeshed in the sound and glorious mysteries,
Reborn and baptized in sleek tone.
Sliding squeaky and sweet on strings with ardor even.
Flames of passion burn around the atman still.

With every breath and note.
Luna stands for the flowers of soul.
Semblances of dreams keep falling like petals,
There are the fantasy and sight.
Plum-Blossoms lay them sacredly in measures of time.

Spirit unwrapped in full state of undress then.
They in prisms of chalices this night.
Acoustical shadow whirls and flits,
The magic buds sprouting,
As if holding all the smiles.

_____

William Yu He graduated from two of the most prestigious law schools in China respectively, also studied in Heidelberg, Cambridge and Harvard. He has already published dozens of Chinese classical poems. Allpoetry.com/William_He

[Kenny Stephens]
Old Cropper's Ridge

Grandpa, take me on that old gravel road
Across cropper's ridge many trips we had made
Down past Sadler's Chapel
On the way to old Bugtussle that little country store
Where I have so many precious memories to this day
I think back on times we spent up at the new ground
Back then people helped each other to set crops in the field
This was my little piece of heaven in those Kentucky Hills
But now it's all gone, it is just a memory
slipping away
It's been so long I can't explain
Since I walked those hollows where I feel
My brothers went before me
I know that's where their heaven is as well
Lord, my soul aches to go back to that little
Farmhouse
Set in the shadow of old Cropper's ridge

———————————

Born March 9 1065
I live in Carroll county Cutler Indiana
Spent summers on Kentucky farm as a child
My passions are nature, fishing, connecting with
spirit and interacting with people.
Allpoetry.com/Kenny_Stephens

[Gary Adcock]

the reunion

as I gazed out on the crowd pondering exactly what to say
the sight of familiar faces for a time took my words away
fifty years had passed since we left the shelter of our school
each so unaware of how life could sometimes be so cruel

I did not see old faces, instead just friends from days gone by
these people gathered in front of me still kids in these old eyes
I did not see the wrinkles nor imperfections age will bring
instead there sat my schoolmates, young as the first day of spring

in the next few hours laughter filled the once silent air
each of us sent back in time when life was lived without a care
people spoke of the old hangouts, movies on a Saturday night
football games and dances, everyone wearing red and white

one never loses High school pride, one never forgets the past
meet many people in our lives but these were meant to last
bonds we make as children, a solid foundation for what's to come
we travel life's winding roads, not forgetting where we're from

as I gazed out on the crowd pondering exactly what to say
the sight of familiar faces for a time took my words away
many years have passed since I had the peace I felt right then
my thanks to each and every one of you, until we meet again

Growing up in the Flint hills of Kansas I have always been a dreamer. I love the outdoors and good music. When you combine the two you have the makings of a great day!
Allpoetry.com/Gary_Adcock

[Manogna Mandadi]

Seeing You as I Do

You don't see yourself the way I do
Maybe that's why I wanna turn into an incredible teacher,
To make you learn the fact that there's nobody as pretty as you.
Because you don't see yourself the way I do
Maybe that's why I crave to blossom into the world's greatest
poet,
To craft a piece of writing that's nearly as beautiful as you.
Because you don't see yourself the way I do
Maybe that's why I long to metamorphose into a non-deceptive
mirror,
To make you see the true blissful essence of your features.
Because you don't see yourself the way I do
Maybe that's why I yearn to evolve into a butterfly
To flutter around a man who makes my heart flutter
Because you don't see yourself the way I do.
Oh, such an astonishing sight you're missing!
I would spend the rest of my life wishing,
For a day to come on which you see yourself the way I do
And whisper to yourself with a gleeful smile 'I love you'.

Manogna Mandadi is an emerging poet and creative writer with a
deep passion for the written word. She holds a degree in Bachelor
of Management Studies from St Francis college for women .
Allpoetry.com/ManognaMandadi

[Stuart Richter]

My lovely

I miss you
How could I have known
It would be the last time
I call your number
So many times
just too hear your voice
And leave you a message
hoping somehow
You hear my words
I feel you close
can smell your cologne
look for you everywhere
hoping, wanting, needing
To be with you
To see you
You cut me deep
Too broken too heal
You were the lovely of my life
just want you to know
I miss you every day
Someday I will
Go beyond the veil
And be with you
My lovely.

I am from Seattle ,WA. I work at a zoo and love to write poetry.
I am married and have three grown daughters and 7
grandchildren. I love to fish and go to the Oregon coast.
Allpoetry.com/The_Traveling_Raven

[Richard F. King]

Anna from the bronx

Under an apricot tree,
I warmed myself
Neath the golden fringe
Of her caress.

Lost in the moment of her
Blue-grey gaze,

I curled like an infant
Before the suckling breasts
She offers,

Alone except for time,
Alone except for passion.

Asking myself,

What bird of heaven
Has lent their plumage
To her winged kiss.

_____

Richard F. King was born In New York city.
Self-raised, self-taught. He does not write,
He remembers. Allpoetry.com/Richking56

[Catherine Mitchell]

Unstoppable Faith

In the depths of despair, I find my soul weighed down,
But within me, an unwavering faith, it is found.
A journey through darkness, a battle to recover,
Yet, in every step I take, I know I will discover.
Dreams that once seemed distant now become clear,
As my spirit awakens and embraces what's near.
Anxieties may assail and fears may try to ensnare,
Yet with bravery as my armor, I rise above despair.
Compassion fuels my heart, guiding each endeavor,
To spread love and kindness, to all souls in need of tender.
Confidence blossoms within me like a mighty tree,
Nurtured by the belief that greater is what I'll be.
Depression may linger, casting shadows all around,
But hope ignites a fire, turning darkness into ground.
In this spiritual dance between struggle and grace,
I find solace in God's presence, where wellness finds its place.
Faith acts as my compass, pointing me towards the light,
A resolute guide through each daunting day and long night.

This journey may be arduous; the path may seem unclear,
Yet with unwavering faith, I face each challenge without fear.

Catherine is from a small town called Ironton, Missouri. When
she is not able to express her thoughts and emotions verbally. She
writes them into poems hoping that it will help others.
Allpoetry.com/Catherine136

[Tim Perkins]

Melody

As a spark of light comes to life in my hand,
Splintered tendrils reach out and draw the air.
Dancing nymphs find new ground and scatter,
Spreading out across the room, creating a rhythm.

As the tune crescendo's, the source gives up its life,
The hand turns cold as the spark flutters and dies.
Like falling soldiers, the dancers in turn,
Bow to their partners, and perform their last show.

And the rhythm is lost to the wind.

I like writing poetry, teaching art and creating stained glass windows. Poetry is the open eye and the searching mind, in a sea of fuzz. Allpoetry.com/Tim_Perkins

[Owen Lester Notaro]

September, Did I Miss Out?

Too big, too small
My body is weird
What fits and feels comfortable?
Spend more
Spend more
I want to wear the emblem of my new team
An emblem of a pillar
Hold me up damn it!
I'll never have anything
These bloody chains of gluttony
Keep me imprisoned
Why do I care what anybody thinks?
Who am I trying to impress?

I retreat to the group
To hide from my insecurities
I'm safe
I'm validated
There's people around me at all times
Still my insecurities find me.
HER
Spend more
Spend more
Damn it!
Emotions exploding like chemicals in a lab

I projectile vomit my feelings
I never see HER again.

A bar in Cambridge
I meet a new muse
To keep me sexually satisfied.
Brighton
Trolley bell rings
Intercourse! Yes!
You strong and intelligent woman
I still want Somerville!
Spend more
Spend more
Damn it!
The one who works at the hospital
Makes me feel so ill
Down by the river,
What is actually happening?
No muggers, lovers, or thieves
Just a madman who wants what he can't have
New people moving into Boston
I'm still here
Another September at home.

————————————

O.L. Notaro is an eccentric and elusive being who lives
somewhere near Boston. He speaks only in metaphors and is
often frustrated. Allpoetry.com/O.L._Notaro

[Robert Jay Cardenas]

To Zona 1894

If only...
my dove
if only
i might offer

the warm glow of dawn's first light
the radiance of joy when i'm with you

the cool diamonds of night
are glittering jewels
to crown you with devotion

the unceasing azure sky
a psalm
to your soul

the moon i would give
to shine about your graceful neck
it belongs to you and no other

the savage storm that lashes out with gales
as i lay down my life for you
defending your honor...your life and happiness

your beautiful body
is a creamy alabaster

your soul is, a morning star
my only religion

if only...
we'd met so long ago
i would've never broken your heart...

like he did

now i take this letter
carefully
i scent it with rose
carefully
i place it beneath
your tombstone

i hope somehow you see my radiant soul burning for you
burning through the darkness of time

—————————————

out of cobwebbed corners of dead dreams
and from the skulls of things i once held faith in
comes the following works
i reach out across time and distance to you
not to be lyrical
or to offer flowery poems. Allpoetry.com/Bakardadea

[Jesse Fenix]

Cigarette Angel

as I walk down a tin-can alley paved with spit
wrinkled walls flash filthy grins
snowy white pigeons, feathery street fog
kaleidoscopic puddles, spirals of neon
tidal waves of sewer steam tapestries
garbage cans overflowing with grey skies,
washed clean by rat tongues

my hair ringed with a cigarette smoke halo
lips glazed with multiple shades of mischief
floral dress winking at the sun
a nicotine Seraphim, fingers stained with gold
rescuing lost shopping carts
filling a beggar's cup with butterflies
leaving behind a trail of perfumed hallelujahs

Jesse Fenix aka Just Poppy is from Massachusetts and enjoys
music, horror movies, zebra finches and writing poetry.
Allpoetry.com/Just_Poppy

[Theresa Gamblin]

Butterfly Wings

There is so much tranquility in movement,
As you watch the wings of a butterfly.
The array of colors is like a peacock feather.
"Twinkling in the light as/they land"
On the petal of a flowers.
"As you witness" and "there is small"
Straw-like tube tongue.
As they fly across sky with each other,
In the simple breeze that blows in summer.
You're watching the breath-taking wings,
Open wide fluttering in flight.
They come in a arrange of different colored,
Wings that change to look fluorescent.
As the movement is so graceful to see,
I feel so grateful to know such beauty exists.

I love to write, and I enjoy poem writing the best. I'm family
person and very close to both side of my family I love writing
because your using imagination allot. I've written ever since I was
a kid. Allpoetry.com/Theresa_Gamblin

[Justice Bevan]

Damned

Love could be written in your voice
Songs of romance danced on your tongue
Tomes filled with magic and wonder
From the whispers your lips uttered

I grasped at all the falling stars
While sitting on the edge of the world
Waiting for you
Star light burns
But not as much as the emptiness that now fills your speech

Waves, swift and mighty
From the oceans that are pulled from the moon
Are calm compared to the pain that crashes deep within
Smiles can hide the pain
But the eyes overflow with it.

You have stained my existence
I was tainted before
Now you have left me darkened
I gasp for air
That isn't here in the space you've left.

I long for starshine warmth
But not the inferno of Helios

You have damned me to the Gods
For only a small taste of Nirvana.

Justice Bevan is from Fort Worth, TX. Poetry had been my lantern in the darkest times of my life. Writing has been a deep passion since I could remember. Allpoetry.com/Justice_Bevan

[Russell Matthew Taunton]
Love Enchanted By Moonlight

I.

Like a pod of baby blue whales ephemeral clouds swim upon a fall gale across oceans of heavenly-sky

Upon a purple swell in the waves of twilight while sweet songbirds take to swiftly winged-flight

Before the consummate black-cloaking finally devours the dying-light thus it paints the covetous contempt begat with onyx-night

Upon golden fields of winter rye lie a lover and his blushing bride as the wise watchful moon slowly comes creeping-past

II.

Underneath a starry-sky when two hearts beat like thunder as stormy-love flashes within their hungry-eyes

In the silky midnight blue the flickers of courting fireflies dot the ebony-hue and love feverishly climaxes in the shimmering-light

Flushed lips upon yearning hips ache desperately to be touched when the burning embers begin to glow so-bright

Glistening bodies must insatiably unite intertwined amidst the sky's black-velvet moonshine

III.

The watchful eyes of a night owl can always tell you all about whoo-hoo

That old man moon has cast his bewitching spell upon these beloveds-too

This magical enchantment never fails to amaze as the hearts of young lovers are set totally blaze whenever two are blissfully falling for love's romantic-gaze

So sweetly tender is the fertile soil's surrender to the fragrant blossoms of passionate love blooming deep within the-night

IV.

While they grow wanderlust as a wild Irish-rose climbing freely to ecstasy upon the early dawning-light

Where the wind softly whispers its lover's secret names filled with fervent desire fanning those all-consuming flames of young love's vain-bonfires

Nevermore shall the unfettered nature of truly enchanted love remain placidly tamed within mankind's unyielding prudish-restrains

---

For: Youth's Young & Wild First Love

I'm an AF Brat & Retired AF/DAV... Born in Italy, part Cherokee, my parents born-raised in the South. I've been writing poetry since the 6th grade. Poetry helps me express myself beyond the ordinary. Allpoetry.com/RustedHalo64

[Mark Anthony Piña]

The Camera Isn't 3

a|She loves me because I know Psychology.
b|They worship her eyes,
a|as I stare into 3...
b|Without sight, a world for you &&& I,
a|just you &&& me.
b|So kiss me with your mind.

c|Tell me that even in Hell,
c|we'd still have Heaven.

———————

♥♥♥ I write my own lyrics & am capable of writing in multiple genres. This is a hobby/passion of mine that will last my lifetime. Allpoetry.com/Mark3pina

[Lisa Fiedor Raines]

Dancing Neon

In the land of
The midnight sun
Far above the
Winter's darkness

Magnetic shimmers
Green and purple
Sun's distant flares
Light the starkness

Graceful curtains
Unseen in the
Never ending
Summer's brightness

As with God's hand
The universe
Paints the world
In its likeness

AlisRamie is from North Carolina, USA.
Interests include: philosophy, history, international relations,
politics, poetry, art, design, jazz, funk, and some good old soul.
Allpoetry.com/AlisRamie

[Yu He]

Reaching Yellow River

Rushing yellow torrents,
Quivering within the wave's intense day.
Wondrous clouds wander,
Shots pan something supernatural,
The story in reality and fantasy in the swing.
In the thunderous roaring tones.
It dinging melodies too.
A Minotaur fiddles in the maze.
On some sandbar ahead,
The slow-sliding reed marshes,
How time has ticked a long take on the brink.

It is older than the flow of human blood.
Chorus that lingers in the ears and mind,
Crystal luster through secret lots.
Bearing centuries' colorful dossier in the stream.
Swimming to a glare of lights at dawn,
Soul grows deep like the river.
When joys have lost their bloom and breath.
What uneasy and what mournful hours.

Whose Aqua of deep woe.
When in disgrace with people's eyes.
Who seeking that beauteous roof to ruin,
Specter shedding scarred fleshes still.
The technicolor synthesizes madness at this point.

Those falling like faint meteor in the gloom,
Brackish with the salt of human tears.
The unfathomable muddiest water is years,
It growing wiser in its ways,
Adolescent in changing moods.

William Yu He graduated from two of the most prestigious law schools in China respectively, also studied in Heidelberg, Cambridge and Harvard. He has already published dozens of Chinese classical poem Allpoetry.com/William_He

[Yu He]

Gaza's Shadow

Here death sleeps not far from them,
Stones that once were a house carrying stories and secrets,
Children's eyes wide open without sin.
For years the cycle has bound them in pain,
A dance of violence with no end to the chain.
The groans of mothers pulsating over and over in the ears.
The trapped mosques make an orchestra of their hunger,
Who will brush off the dead leaves,
The life constantly wears its black dress.
Gods play dice once again,
Sparing a thought for the indifference,
Reconciling offenders and making Justice drop her angry rod.

The wounds are turning into a kind of weaponry in a flash,
The world wondering what led them astray,
Endless dirge distilling a distinct urge.
Gaza In Lens flying high with no sound,
Tunnels anger revenge blood oaths burn,
Allah should have power to stop this troublesome people here,
Though Solomon's Temple gone from sight its memory bright,
When sorrow strikes the ground,
A tale of conflict, suffering and hopes.
Crumbling with the weight,
In tiny cracks along the sacred wall,
People are reading their Mincha-prayer in the mournful tones.

William Yu He graduated from two of the most prestigious law schools in China respectively, also studied in Heidelberg, Cambridge and Harvard. He has already published dozens of Chinese classical poem Allpoetry.com/William_He

[Allix Dg]

Silent Goodbye

They will see us waving from such great heights

Winkling my fingertips
I float
Drifting softly
Imagining your excitement
A silent goodbye

One day you'll look up to Daddy
Who am I to leave you hanging?

───────────────

Boxes is a heavy equipment mechanic from Vancouver, BC. His work currently focuses on challenging social commentary. For a hearty winter mac & cheese try adding a can of cream of chicken soup! Allpoetry.com/Boxes

[Matthew Broughton]

Dreaded Departure

Everything from my collected memories flashed before my eyes.
All replaying in slow motion of my last moments before...
throwing my soul into the abyss.

I did this without forgiveness! My regrets... rewards my wrong-
doing and failed promises. I have broken more hearts than
records. I been cursed and betrayed by the pen and sword.
I was a passionate-ambitious dreamer with epiphanies, that the
richest person could not afford

The void of whiteness.
Is this my new home?
The wrath of this dying world. Scares me more than any failure.
If only my efforts spared me from karma, now facing multiple
decisions, tools to construct my path. I choose to bring forth my
demise.

I chose to follow this path. I tie faults of no kind. I blamed anyone
and everyone. When I was the one! Condemn anyone around,
you for what sake?

What would you give or take?
To find peace within my eternal absence?
Is that how, you wish to remember me?

My spirits spreading to corners of the world, all calling out to
reach me. The weight of consciousness decreasing, unable to

vividly, and physically express concerns that are no longer part of my being.

People whom entered my life from the past to my final moment... fill my eyes along with tears, I could no longer restrain

Whom to thought emotions, existed in a place, where colors radiate differently, with reminders in between highlighting other experiences.

  Now, they all surround me for the last goodbye.
Not the reunion, a peace bringer would slay for. Where we cannot touch or exchange feelings through words.

My magic will live on!
Ever more so, even if my essence expires.

I've searched for solace.

I've even conspired against time
God made it prominent.

To search beyond....

the means of obtainable comfort.
To live by the word and serve light.

Remember my voice
One day, you may not hear it anymore

Remember my touch....

All you'll have left to
remember me by is the wind....

I lived to immortalize our values
When our values could have immortalized us....

I lived to bring all of you to life!
Nonetheless....

mine was treated
like it's a game
My life is not fit
For a book or frame
"The More I Remember; The More I forget. "
De Ja Vu daily reminders.
Everything still feels different
Yet, it's all the same

This life meant to be.
Was never meant for me.
Mindless self-indulgence.
Just another memory.

Is there more after this purpose?
I am not absolutely certain.
No room, for troubling questions.

My apologies for being a burden.

——————————————

#Proud Father #Author #Poet #Health&FitnessAdvocate
#StoryTeller #Healing-Writer #Inspirational Speaker #Certified
Anti-HumanTraffickingAdvocate
Allpoetry.com/Matthew_Descovia

[Lisa Fiedor Raines]

You are God's Child

I see the love in your eyes
You feel my heart

You are the calm and the peace
So pure is your soul

You don't see through me
You see me

All you need do is smile
And I am comforted

There is God beaming
Through your being

To be close to you
Is to feel the love of God

———————————

AlisRamie is from North Carolina, USA.
Interests include: philosophy, history, international relations,
politics, poetry, art, design, jazz, funk, and some good old soul.
Allpoetry.com/AlisRamie

[Jim Beitman]
I see their faces

I see their faces
some will never be returned
'kidnapped' posters fade

––––––––––––––

I am an artist living in Noblesville Indiana. Writing is a great
media that helps distill my feelings, thoughts, and experiences. It
is always a great thrill to be included in an Allpoetry anthology!
Allpoetry.com/Beitmanjim

[Jarvis M. Giles II]

Dear Gaza

Well, there may come a time where he may have a chance, let me
run through this and give you a glance.

That for over seventy-five years the American's have been allies,
with home of Israel and help protect their land and skies.

Now tragedy has happened, and Gaza must pay, for whatever
they were thinking, I truly must say.

That Gaza must have lost some marbles up-stairs, now look at
your streets or the ones that were once there.

Because the Prime Minister of Israel just took them all out, to take
Americans hostage you must want to shout.

From the hole you are hiding in deep in a cave, Biden has
unleashed us, now Gaza will never be saved!

There is nowhere to run and nowhere to hide, Gaza you really
missed up and he is still not my guy.

But to take the hostages that call America home, your death
sentence awaits, and there is nowhere to roam.

Because my guy or not, Biden still knows his role, don't mess up
with Israel or we will be in the hole.

Just like you, Gaza but we'll way better equipped, man you better
drink up and enjoy every sip.

Because you are now cut off from my family of God, your
buildings are destroyed and your streets now show rods.

Of the rebar that once held your concrete together, Gaza, is no
more people they are destroyed now forever.

So better hide well Gaza somewhere safe in the hills, Hell what am

I saying, you will never match up to our Seals.
That are probably their now and looking for clues, so, farewell
dear Gaza because you now are screwed.

A simple guy from Turnerville, Alabama who was raised to have a
proper code, morals and respect . And that if you want something
you get yourself out there and work for it, nothing is free
Allpoetry.com/Marvelousjarvis

[Patricia M Batteate]

My Siblings

Growing up at a time
Before the PC and video game
We once had block parties
And knew everyone's name

Raised in our family home
With one sister and four brothers
Every night we sat down for dinner
No different than any other

My parents were fair yet firm
They raised us all to be honest
Fibbing was never an excuse
Your word was considered a promise

All of my siblings are extraordinary
Creatively brilliant with a touch of humor
Scholars and athletes were positively promoted
Our generation was post baby boomer

The oldest is Norman, voted ASB president
After Berkely, The Peace Corp and Court clerk
He studied to become a Culinary Chef
Where to this day he achieves his best work

Dennis, the Cowboy
Following the family tradition
The original "Horse Whisperer"
And the greatest jockey there's ever been

Kathleen my only sister
Mother, Wife and holds a career
An immigration specialist at Livermore labs
Her family she holds so dear

Daniel Jr. named after dad
Who died at a young age
It seems like only yesterday
We have yet to turn the page

The youngest, his name is Vince
He joined the minors to play ball
He went on to follow in dad's footsteps
Cryogenic engineering his call

There is no way to choose
To single out one sibling without the others
My admiration and love are evenly felt
For my sister and each of my brothers

I feel so blessed being born at a time
Where the family unit thrived
Innocence was preserved
And praise God for the gift of life

Born and raised in the San Francisco Bay Area. I found a career as an engineer. A quote from Nightbird: 'You can't wait till life is easy to decide when to be happy'
Allpoetry.com/Patricia_Batteate

[Madelyn Paine]

Halloween

Walking through the night
Blood red sky glowing bright
Dressed as zombies and knights
Oh, It's Halloween night... Halloween night....Halloween night

Goblins, Zombies, and mummies too
The skeletons dance around
Witches zooming around on their brooms
Oh, you better watch out tonight
It's Halloween night... Halloween night.....Halloween night

trick or treating is so much fun
Candy Corn, kit-kats, and chocolate bars oh my
going door to door
On Halloween night

The darkness hides secrets in the night
You better watch out for witches, vampires, and Frankenstein too
Go up to the doors asking for sweets
We tiptoe across lawns tripping over candy wrappers
Oh, it's Halloween night....Halloween night.... Halloween night

HALLOWEEN NIGHT!!

I'm a high school student in Canton, Michigan. I find great
happiness in poetry. I love expressing my interests and feelings
through my poems to share with others! Allpoetry.com/Poet369

[Lisa Fiedor Raines]

Heart Failure is Not a Failure of Heart

I may be old and tired, and
My body may be broken down, but
My heart has not failed

If I cannot make it to
The front lines, I will
Hold the line at home

Our diversity is our strength, and
We can be the nation we believe in
We must not lose our faith in Spirit

———————————

AlisRamie is from North Carolina, USA.
Interests include: philosophy, history, international relations,
politics, poetry, art, design, jazz, funk, and some good old soul.
Allpoetry.com/AlisRamie

[Stephen Harris]
The Yorkshire Tongue

Yorkshire is where you will find real people
tired and grounded, well-worn people
where the dialect isn't just spoken
but is beaten, chiseled and hammered
by the tongue and the tools of the mining trade

it is the talk of a fair but hard-faced folk
long since crafted in candlelit mines
where there was no time for the twee faint tones
between pickaxe swings, guttural cries
and the rasping coughs of coal-dust splutterings

here they speak as they are, bluntly and plainly
sometimes wielding words like an offending smack
tiny granite tablets quarried without filter
feeding by force the familiar and foreign ear
with a wit drier than their own drowning pits

I am 54 and based in Wakefield, West Yorkshire. Poetry, both in
its reading and writing brings me so much pleasure and I hope
any of mine you may read will do the same for you.
Allpoetry.com/Atryst

[Samantha Kriese]

Night's Decorum

The night is her house,
carefully placing her garland of stars.
The sun is disinterested in her art,
but the moon loves it so.
Until the pearl of night grows dull,
she will bedizen the sky.

S. A. Kriese resides in Chippewa Falls, Wisconsin. She is the author of 'One Who Plays with Paper and Pens' and 'In the Black Inkwell.' She has been featured in seven anthologies. 18 years of writing. Allpoetry.com/S.A.Kriese

[Cassandra Rey]

Butterflies in my Stomach

Butterflies in my stomach,
not knowing where to start.
Searching for something
I lost long ago.
Wanting more than anything
to go back in time,
Dreaming about the girl
Lost in my mind.
Crying for help,
I've tried and I've tried
not hard enough
there's nothing to find.

HarryPotterGeek is from American Fork, Utah. She enjoys
Reading, writing and doing puzzles, and loves doing puzzles.
Allpoetry.com/HarryPotterGeek

[William Morris Thurston III]
Flowers

A flower seemed sweetest when found on Market, not a store but
a street, way back in 1972.

She could've been Minnie Rippertin's daughter. She looked like
Minnie, smiled like Minnie, wore tiny flowers in her hair like
Minnie and had the sweetest singing voice just like Ms. Minnie
too, but she was only 13 years young like me.

I watched this flower's blossoms bloom as The Commodores
"JUST TO BE CLOSE TO YOU" watered the grounds to that of
which my love for a flower grew.

O' my love,
my young black love,
my first love,
my first real love,
it's so strange these days how the seasons change,
and how my love for this flower still remains!

———————————

My Mother, Bless Her Heart, is the first inspiration when came to
Poetry, for She herself was a Poet. She's my Latest and my
Greatest Inspiration and will always be! Allpoetry.com/Poet-
BillyRayMorris

[Alwyn Barddylbach]

Oh Mel!

Sweet and sour
sherbet dips
meets mischief
effervescence
lollipops

Imagination is
in a child's heart
except for
Miss Allsorts...

Hers is on her lips.

Candy store now open!

———————————

Mel can be very self-absorbed chomping her away through
Barddylbach's Crazy Crystal Candy Store - AB Blue Mountains
Allpoetry.com/Barddylbach

[Sharon Diaz]

Scarlet & P-U-L-S-E

Smooth, present
The vagarious route - dark and promiscuous
The night... tumultuous
My eyes wander around her....I love her, her skin, the seditious
cut...

Manly, robust, impressive,
It heightens me...
Hands that touch me willingly
...The door was wildly open- our home

Our hearts were dancing with the rhythm-bright angels and saints
welcomed us, enchantingly...
I awoke from this dream....I heard screams, I heard tears falling, I
heard the scarlet red gripping
the floor's cracks and fissures
That laugh,
Dominating every breath, every impulse to live...
To stand by...
I grasped her hand, tightly...my life depends on this grip...
Do not let go, my love...
Don't let go...

Sharon was born and raised in Puerto Rico. Lives in the Sunshine State of Florida. She is an English professor, beach enthusiast, and animal lover. For her poetry is 'the rhythm of life'.
Allpoetry.com/Norahs_Zaid

[Tina Thrower]

What is love?

Love is a rainbow with many shapes and colors
some light and bright as could be
dark and gloomy like the moonlight shining brightly upon us at
night fall and dark cold night,
never understanding the clear intense harmony of love,
an everlasting effect you never quite get over or would want to
really.

_____

My world - I'm a mother and grandma, love the great outdoors,
bowling, watching movies and going on walks. I'm mainly just
trying to live one day at a time. Allpoetry.com/Icygreenleopard4

[Robert J Owens]

Meg

You were my first crush when I was 15
You were 28, a Goddess, and a Queen

With your jet black hair and exquisite beauty
So exotic and erotic together we'd be melodic

In an imperfect world with the perfect intentions
Meg Tilly you're the charm that this prince has been missing

So all hail the Queen the girl in a swing
Who still captivates me even as KING 👑.

Dedicated to Margaret Elizabeth Chan A.K.A
Meg Tilly ♟

Krownroyal007 is from Los Angeles CA and has always had a love
for poetry and song writing and would very much like to write a
whole book of poems and create a beautiful and respected body of
work . Allpoetry.com/Krownroyal007

[Melissa Davilio]

Into the Forest

The creaking of the pines
elicits icy shivers,
like steel fingers
raked upon a naked spine,
pine needles quivering,
jagged splinters
jabbed into desperate
thirsty veins

Slivers of pain,
slices of sorrow,
glimpsed through the gaping cracks
between the bark,
as stark winds whisper
then wail
weaving twisted tales
of ennui and despair

Oh, the horrors they have seen
while the sun giggles and gleams
from her corner of the forest
peering from her perch
amid the heavens,
her cackles seep into the earth
to settle
among the dirt and the decay

As the emerald canopy
leads the lost souls astray
through the labyrinth
of decomposing leaves,
corpses cast off from the trees,
disrobing before the fastidious eyes
of their maker,
undertakers laying out their palls
for the weak and broken to bear

_____

Melissa Davilio is a self-taught poet residing in Thomaston, CT, USA with her husband and their furry family. She is domestic violence awareness advocate, a treehugger, and an animal lover. Allpoetry.com/MyriadMusings

[Courtney Weaver Jr.]

Unwavering Defiance

The strongest boy in our high school
Stood proud and tall, his long blond hair
Flowing like a lion's mane, untouched
By the discipline of sports.

The coaches, with their worn-out bodies
And bitter eyes, despised him
For his defiance, for his refusal
To conform to their standards.
They could not cage his spirit,
Could not tame his wildness.

He held the iron cross with ease,
His muscles quivering with strength
As he defied gravity, defied the teachers
Who stood by, powerless and envious.
We watched in awe, as he defied
Their expectations, their limitations.

He was a rebel in a world of conformity,
A lone wolf in a pack of sheep
And we, his fellow students, admired
His courage, his defiance, his refusal
To be like everyone else.

In those moments, as he held the iron cross,
We saw something beyond physical strength;
We saw a spirit that could not be broken,
A resilience that could not be tamed.
And as he fell to the mats,
We knew that he would rise again,
Stronger than before.

In our identical blue gym shorts,
With our last names scrawled across our chests,
We were all the same, except for him.
He was a symbol of resistance,
A beacon of hope for those who dared
To defy the constraints of society.

I had faith he could rise from the dead,
Not in a religious sense, but in a way
That spoke to his indomitable spirit.
He was the strongest boy in our high school,
Not because of his physical prowess,
But because of his unwavering defiance
And the unyielding strength of his soul.

—————————————

I am 66-year-old male born and raised in New Orleans. Writing
poetry helps me make sense of the things that happen in everyday
life. Allpoetry.com/Gray0328

[Maxwell Sebastian Burchett]

Black Swans

Black swans are a thing.
That thing never seen before,
Not known to exist,
What has never happened before.

If you can think of it,
Can expect or imagine it,
That swan is not black, or a swan,
Just a strange possibility.

I discovered my own personal swans,
Surprised by, not discovered,
Personal tsunamis, personal lottery wins,
Not the Vegas kind; rather, the lotteries of life.

Never imagined things I might do
Or would happen while racing into eternity.
Is the incredible waiting to spring?
What will it mean for me, or you?

Wonderfully good, or bad beyond belief?
Shocks of the universe or just for your life?
Intimate black swans while on your way,
The chance encounter changing life.

Unknown unknowns.
No need to worry.
Can't do anything about
A new wrinkle in what in life cannot expect.

The unexpected we can never know
Until fate dishes it out.
Destiny that was there all along,
A high or low note of life's song.

_____

Max Burchett: a writer, singer and songwriter,
A crooner, a teller of tales,
A dream maker, soul shaker and captivator,
Hoping that in verse and prose he prevails.
Allpoetry.com/MaxBurchett

[Kirsty MacKinnon Leese]
deciduous.

you crackle in my mouth
effervescent
between my teeth
stuck in places
I could reach
if I wanted to.

you taste of mangoes -
delicious fables
ripe and unfamiliar
dancing down my tongue
in foreign flavours
soaked with gold.

dangerous thing,
wild and fruitful.
I hold your gaze
with wide-eyed innocence
until your edges curl
in fiddleheads.

you feel like spring
yet smell of autumn,
crisp and fading.
I bite your flesh

chewing slowly
and dream of stolen summers.

Selkirsty is a writer and poet based in Scotland's Outer Hebrides.
A keen naturalist, she draws her inspiration from her wild love of
people and nature. Allpoetry.com/selkirsty

[Sindy Mitchell]

The Wind

A gust of wind was gasping among the yellow fog,
Rain plummeting on my drenched trench coat,
I race down the deserted street with trembling feet,
He was there leaning on a flickering lamp post,
His dark, disheveled hair clung to his damp face,
With downcast eyes he mumbled nocuous words,
A siren screeches at a distant tavern,
Shadows of the night start swirling in my mind,
My heart tinged as my legs quaked,
Tears drippled down my rosy cheeks,
His body disappeared as the lumichron clock strikes midnight.

Seasons pass,
As the wintry blizzard melts into a puddle of tears,
I grow old,
The hourglass figure flees as the robin escapes from the shrike,
A ray of light glimmers outside my windowpane.

A gentle breeze sways my kempt hair in the moonlight,
The face of the moon beams with exuberance,
Solar lights glisten as wine glasses cling to the melodies of the
evening revel,
The crowd chatters of Michelangelo,
The sweet aroma of my flowery dress adds flavor to the air,
As the air caresses my skin,
A dark, sturdy figure slowly strolls towards me,

His tender eyes so full of wit and rigor,
He whispers sweet tunes in my ear,
He held my hand and we danced in the night sky,
And the compassionate breeze circled us among the twinkling
stars.

Sindy Mitchell enjoys teaching children and playing music. She
graduated from the University of Toronto and has a master's
degree. Never give up hope for a better future.
Allpoetry.com/S._Mitchell

[Darron Baker]

The Wolves Are Coming

Here I lay my head,
Waiting for the next day,
How long must I wait,
For I must keep the wolves at bay.

Their teeth flashing,
claws scratching,
Weapons at the ready,
Grip firm as steel,
Eyes searching for peril.

Yellow eyes all round,
Staring back at me,
Ready to begin their assault.

So I wait in anticipation
For the battle to begin,
The vicious struggle,
To declare a winner in the end.

I must win several times,
My enemies need only once,
Every blow counts,
Moving to finality,
Till darkness finally comes.

Darron Baker is from Valdosta, GA. Poetry helps me express
emotions, and to ponder questions about life
Allpoetry.com/Darronbaker468

[Tina Thrower]

1qa to 2qa Family Tree

Plowdog,

Plowdog,

Plowdog..

plow me a Field of Dreams...

Make it 6ft.deep and 12 ft. wide ;

Because you know now WHO I AM...

Plowdog come see me ASAP...

I Sure miss u too; Before u know I will be there Plowdog too.

Plowdog said to Plowdog "I love u to the moon and back.

My world - I'm a mother and grandma, love the great outdoors, bowling, watching movies and going on walks.I'm mainly just trying to live one day at a time. Allpoetry.com/Icygreenleopard4

Printed in Great Britain
by Amazon

38193105R00106